OPENING TO GOD

Guided Imagery Meditation on Scripture

Completely Revised and Expanded

CAROLYN STAHL BOHLER

UPPER
ROOM BOOKS
Nashville

OPENING TO GOD
Copyright © 1996 by Carolyn Stahl Bohler
All rights reserved.

No part of this book may be reproduced in any manner whatsoever without written permission of the publisher except in brief quotations embodied in critical articles or reviews. For information, address The Upper Room, 1908 Grand Avenue, P.O. Box 189, Nashville, Tennessee 37202-0189.

Scripture quotations not otherwise identified are from the New Revised Standard Version of the Bible, copyright 1989 by the Division of Christian Education of the National Council of the Churches of Christ in the USA and are used by permission.

All scripture quotations designated *The Complete Gospels* are taken from *The Complete Gospels: Annotated Scholars Version.* Copyright © 1992, 1994 by Polebridge Press. Used with permission. All rights reserved.

Cover design: Kris Ellisor
First Printing: March 1996 (7)
ISBN: 0-8358-0768-1
Library of Congress Catalog Card Number: 95-62356

Printed in the United States of America

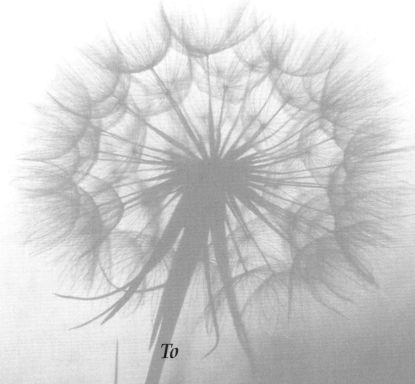

To

Marilyn Collins, my twin sister,

with whom I share past and future images

and much love,

And to

Mary Nell and Bob Bohler, my in-laws,

who exemplify the ministry of the laity

CONTENTS

Foreword

❋

Good news! Carolyn Stahl Bohler has rewritten a very good book, making this edition even better! If you are looking for a succinct introduction to the creative use of biblical imaging, meditation, and imaging prayer in your own life and/or in your work, this is it! Many of us, like the author, have discovered the healing, growth-nurturing power that becomes available when we use stories and guided imaging in our counseling, teaching, and personal struggles for wholeness. This book guides the reader through the basic steps of using fifty biblical stories and images as open channels of this therapeutic energy. The process of opening to God described in these pages is a way of using the imagination to release the flow of this spiritual power.

In addition to the obvious usefulness of biblical imaging in pastoral care and counseling, Professor Bohler shows how they also are growth tools in other dimensions of ministry. These include religious education, spiritual direction, and worship. The guided meditations in these pages are made more useful both by detailed instructions concerning how to use them and by the scholarly knowledge she shares about the biblical stories on which they focus.

Clearly the author's wide experience in teaching and her use of guided biblical imaging in her professional life during the two decades since the first edition's publication has enriched this edition. Her years of personal experience and family living have enhanced her application of these methods to the everyday problems and possibilities people face day by day. Furthermore, her journeying in the Christian lifestyle has deepened both her heart-level and head-level understanding of the process of enabling spiritual healing and growth.

I rejoice that the author's message has a robust, prophetic power. She expresses a keen awareness of the crucial justice and environmental

issues in society that impact all our personal and family problems profoundly, for better or for worse. Women's stories and female biblical
images like Mary and Martha, Ruth, the widow's gift, the woman baking
bread, and the caring love of a mother hen are illuminated by her insights
about the special challenges and opportunities women face in our male-
dominated society.

Reading Carolyn Bohler's insightful book reinforces my long-held
conviction that teachers are among the most fortunate people in the world.
Full credit for this valuable volume belongs to her, of course, not to her
former mentors like myself. But to witness and learn from this clear evidence of her growing intellectual and spiritual journey is indeed a source
of joy. This joy is increased by my expectation that this recreated book
will be a valuable resource to many other spiritual searchers on their
journeys. My hope and prayer is that it will enable you to discover that
opening to God is also a way of opening to the riches of your deeper self
and equally important, to deepening relationships with those you love.

—HOWARD CLINEBELL

Preface

❀

Ecause two decades have passed since the first publication of this book, the revised and expanded edition is to a great extent rewritten. During this time, I have served as the minister of the Mission Hills United Methodist Church in San Diego, California and, for fourteen years, as Professor of Pastoral Theology and Counseling at United Theological Seminary in Dayton, Ohio. As I have led guided imagery meditations on scripture, participants' feedback has enriched my understanding of the diverse phenomena people experience. Also, in these two settings lay persons, clergy colleagues, and seminary students have told me how they used these meditations. With the hope that their experience will spark new ideas for readers, I present some of their creative uses.

Chaplain Dr. Gail Paul used these meditations with the inmates at Garner Correctional Institution, a high security prison for men in Newtown, Connecticut, to facilitate spiritual growth as well as healing around social and psychological issues.[1] The Reverend Cynthia Stackpole, clergy person in New York, led twelve nursing home residents, each over eighty years old, in Bible study, using guided imagery. Her husband, Rick, also a clergyperson, has used these meditations in a variety of camp settings and camp staff meetings. Tracey Taylor-Kunst, a Christian educator in Michigan, cofacilitated the practice of these meditations for a six-week adult church school class. She has also used them as devotionals for church meetings and at staff retreats.

Professor of Religious Studies, Dennis Doyle, a Roman Catholic, used these meditations as part of his personal devotions "during a period of great stress" when his four sons were quite young. At that time he started with Meditation 1 and worked his way through all the meditations in order. Later, after his father died, he adapted some of the meditations in order to meet and talk with his father in his imagination. He called both experiences "emotionally liberating."

Dr. Sharon Showman, a United Methodist clergywoman who teaches communication at Bluffton College in Ohio, tells me that she uses these meditations at holiday times with music in the background to focus and to receive feedback. The meditations become a companion to Bible study, with the Bible as the focus on the Word and the meditation as the focus on what is happening within. She also leads others in these meditations at women's sharing groups, youth and adults retreats, and sparingly in worship when appropriate.

Sallie Bailey, an Episcopal priest, and Carole Wood, a United Methodist pastor, met regularly as spiritual friends while they were in seminary. One of them led the other in a guided meditation when they met; the next meeting they reversed roles. The Reverend Ms. Bailey told me of a time later in her ministry when, as the chaplain of a retirement home, she visited a seventy-three-year old woman. The older woman had not been raised in the church and said she didn't know Jesus but wanted to. Chaplain Bailey led the woman in a guided meditation during which the woman responded, "I met him! I met Jesus!" The woman asked to receive baptism, and she often referred to that first encounter with Jesus.

After the publication of the earlier edition of this book, I discovered that people expected me to be a spokesperson for imagery meditation above all other forms of prayer. Then and now, I hold that this is but one of a variety of dynamic options for prayer. In a second book, *Prayer on Wings: A Search for Authentic Prayer*, I examined five styles of prayer: action, imagery, discourse, silence, and repeated phrases. Imagery prayer is but *one* of these five styles. It does not suit everyone. Some people prefer prayer using words, silence, or short phrases that they repeat again and again. Nor is imagery recommended as the only style of prayer for those who do find it valuable. Its usefulness comes in connection with silence, reflection, and action. Imagery does remain one of the most exciting forms of prayer, a marvelous option for people in groups, especially small groups.

I confess that I have more interest in the Bible than I did eighteen years ago. The more I have learned from teachers and colleagues, the more I realize what a radical anthology the Bible is. I now experience more connection with the people we find in the scriptures—their God-wrestlings and human struggles. Some of these struggles include widespread oppression, which we continue to have today. The Bible contains many difficult, almost unbearable, stories and passages, as well as stories of heroes. We cannot find an "answer" in the Bible in order to apply it to today—even if we wanted to—without understanding the cultures of ancient times, Jesus' day, *and* today! Therefore, we need to learn about all these cultures and keep learning. Consequently, in this edition I have given more attention to the scripture passage and its context. Now you may use the meditations for some Bible study as well as prayer. For those who want to preach from one of these passages, the biblical notes provide beginning research.

I restrained myself from making time-bound comments about the application of a particular biblical passage to my present political or cultural context in order to give this book a longer life.

In this volume I added twenty new meditations to the original thirty of the first edition. I have maintained the order of the original thirty, interspersing the new ones with the original ones. I did not delete any of the original meditations; I rewrote many, retitled others.

Chapters 1 and 2 are new. The first provides background for the psychological and religious use of imagery. The second conveys theological reflection upon how we receive guidance or revelation from God. Chapter 3 presents the practical matters of preparing, practicing, and debriefing these meditations.

The word *practice* has two meanings. In one sense, a person practices to improve or to get ready for an event. A pianist practices to prepare for a performance. In the other sense of the word, practice is the process of doing something regularly. The nurse practices medicine. We practice hospitality; we practice prayer. In this edition when I refer to practicing a meditation, I use the word *practice* with the second meaning. I do not mean to rehearse the meditation but rather to do the meditation. In the first edition I consistently used the word *do*, but now I prefer to emphasize the process, the practice of it.

Unless it is otherwise noted, biblical citations at the beginning of each meditation are from The New Revised Standard Version. Frequently for the Gospel passages, I have preferred the translation found in *The Complete Gospels: Annotated Scholars Version*. However, since most readers would not have this resource, I have cited *The Complete Gospels* sparingly.

In the scripture printed at the first of each meditation, I do not change any gender pronouns referring to God. The New Revised Standard

Version is an improvement over past translations in this regard. (*An Inclusive Language Lectionary* is even better, but it only includes lectionary passages and is not used as often.) However, God's self-revelation is enjoyable and surprising. While meditating you may experience God, Jesus, Ruth, Wisdom, or any other symbol in brand new ways. In fact, I highly encourage exploration!

Two people have been especially helpful to me in the preparation of this edition. My husband John edited the work not only with an eye to clarity and grammar, but also as one who cares how the Bible is read. Martha Anderson, our faculty administrative assistant, finalized the printed copy, often providing encouragement in the process.

1

Imagery

Purposes and Effects of Imagery

IMAGERY MEDITATION SERVES three primary purposes: to enjoy the richness of the experience, to become aware of your current state, and to aim toward a particular goal. Recollect or anticipate a gorgeous sunset, a delicious fondue, or a strong hug of love. Those images enrich your present experience, no matter what else they also do.

Or consider leaving work after an exhausting stint of overtime, trying to decide whether to visit your mother in the nursing home or to take a nap. You hear yourself as you casually say to a friend, "I'm *hanging on by a thread.*" That *image*—if you pay attention to it—tells you your current state. It could guide you as you choose to get rest first, then visit your mother.

Maybe you are about to return to church after an illness, ride a bike twenty miles, or ask a friend to the movies. You have a goal, so you visualize yourself doing it, rehearsing it in your mind. The visualization not only motivates you; it gathers your energies toward achieving that goal.[1]

Guided imagery meditation on scripture, while similar to these familiar uses of imagery, has more structure and intentionally relates to the Judeo-Christian tradition. As one practices the meditation "A Little Cloud of Hope," one may observe the inexpressible beauty of the horizon with a tiny cloud puff barely visible. Although that person may never figure out any particular "meaning" for the horizon or cloud in his daily life, he could simply enjoy the scene. It's beautiful, period. His exposure to that beauty enlarges his sense of being. This exemplifies the first purpose of imagery: simply to enjoy the richness of the experience.

If while practicing the meditation "Finding a Buried Treasure" a person discovers a diploma under some heavy rocks, she may be made more aware that "education" is of value, perhaps hard to get and with "heavy" obligations but nevertheless important. That image illustrates the second purpose of imagery: a discovery about a current state. In this case, practicing the meditation leads to her underscoring her high regard for education.

The third purpose for imagery is obvious when one practices the meditation "Expanding a Quality." One may choose to liken the leaven to a particular quality one wants to develop; in this case, decisiveness. One then visualizes oneself throughout a day's activities being decisive—standing up for beliefs, making decisions clearly. With this use of the imagination, one aims toward a particular goal—that of developing the quality of decisiveness.

In the children's book *Frederick* by Leo Lionni, Frederick is a field mouse who lives with other mice along the farmer's wall. These mice gather corn, nuts, wheat and straw; but Frederick isn't working, or so it seems to the others. Frederick protests: "I gather sun rays for the cold dark winter days. . . . I gather colors, for winter is gray." He gathers words, for they'll run out of things to say.

Winter comes. The mice huddle, eat, and grow weary of cold and talking. Eventually they ask Frederick for *his* supplies. So Frederick invites them to close their eyes. Then he speaks to them of the sun's rays. The mice begin to feel warmer. He tells them of blue periwinkles, red poppies in the yellow wheat, and green leaves of the berry bush. His fellow workers see the colors vividly in their minds.

This children's book combines the three purposes of imagery. Those who are willing and able to observe, remember, and imagine are gifted people (or mice) indeed. Not only do the images enrich their own lives, but the sharing of these images can actually help others.

"It's so real" exclaims the person awaking from a dream. "I was sure we could do it," gasps the teammate as she reaches the finish line of the relay race. Whether we visualize healing until it manifests, live "as if" we were tolerant until we are, or repeat while climbing the mountain, "I think I can. I think I can. I think I can," imagination affects events.

Psychologist Carl Jung used *active imagination* with his clients because he knew the effect it could have upon their lives. Unlike some of his predecessors, he perceived that individuals could work with their own imagery. He trusted people to grasp possible meanings and to weave the meanings together to gain wisdom regarding their emotions or behaviors. Imagination comes not only from one's intuitions and so-called "internal" images but also from sensations in the external world. The therapist joins with clients as a helping partner. But only the one who imagines knows intimately the connection between internal intuitions and external sensations or events.[2]

Although the most well-known, Jung was not the first modern psychologist to use mental imagery. In the late nineteenth and early twentieth centuries, Sir Francis Galton and Alfred Benet were pioneers in this work. Carl Happich, a German doctor, developed a method of suggesting predetermined scenes such as a meadow, a mountain, or a chapel to initiate imagery sessions in his work with clients. His goal was spiritual integration.[3]

A number of approaches to guided imagery in therapy developed. Robert DeSoille's method became known as the "Directed Daydream," an approach I find quite compatible with the meditations in this book. This method suggests images while allowing individuals the freedom to visualize details. Persons may find their own insights without always needing interpretation from a guide or therapist.

Consider a person diagnosed with cancer, diabetes, or AIDS. How she or he currently imagines the disease can affect the outcome of treatment. Is the disease "invading," as a thief; "fighting," as a soldier; "decaying," as a leaf; or "tarnishing," as a metal exposed to air? Becoming aware of that current image about the disease is helpful.

Taking another step, persons—perhaps with the help of a pastor, counselor, or medical expert—can develop a set of images that help them envision health, vitality, and recovery (if that is the goal). One person can imagine his body's catching and evicting the "thief" with the help of the bloodstream. Another might enlist the immune system's additional guards to defend against the "fight." A third might allow the leaf to "decay" until new life emerges, healthy in the next season. Or one can imagine the chemotherapy and radiation as polishing off the "tarnish," permitting a natural shine.[4] The imaging helps mobilize the will and energize the body. Just as crucial, the imaging helps people feel like—and be—participants in their own treatment.

The imagination is a critical element of moral living. We "see" the possible consequences of our attitudes and behavior before we commit ourselves to stands and action. We "envision" better ways. While many imagine war as the solution to a crisis, a small group of prophetic people who pray may *imagine* turning swords into plowshares and spears into pruning hooks.

Peculiarly, the imagination can "stretch" from an apparently trivial event to the most profound.[5] To illustrate, you might practice "The Announcement of Birth through You" from this book. You could gain a sense that the "birth" to which you are being called is that of taking a strong stand on a vital moral issue. In the midst of that meditation, you notice that the birth announcement is on light green paper. Ah, light green—the color for which you have been searching to paint your bedroom. You can take the stand *and* paint your bedroom green.

Medical science recognizes two types of brain function. The left hemisphere (for the majority of people) largely controls our ability to use language, mathematics, and logic, while the right controls musical ability, recognition of visual patterns, and the expression of emotion.[6]

I believe God reveals wisdom through all that we are as created beings. It is reasonable to believe that our prayer, our opening to God, includes our whole brain! Yet Christians often have limited prayer to language. Using imagery, persons enlist the right hemisphere of the brain (for right-handed persons), perhaps strengthening its capabilities. Imagery evokes emotions and sensations as an integral part of the prayer itself.

Perhaps for this reason, imagery meditation is especially helpful with persons who are grieving or are in some other type of transition in their life. They cannot continue exactly as they were—circumstances or personal, familial, or community maturation make change necessary. They have to get out of the set behavior and attitudes that served them well in earlier situations. They literally have to imagine a different way to behave and to approach their situations.

I do not recommend imagery without qualified supervision for persons who have a hard time differentiating external reality from internal images. These persons may need to focus attentively to the "real" world of events. I would not advise imagery for people who frequently live in their daydreams but have difficulty implementing action. Whereas most people avoid imagery and imagination and attend to their behaviors (actions), those who live a great deal in their fantasy may need to pay more attention to their actions.

IMAGERY PRAYER/IMAGERY MEDITATION

TO MANY PEOPLE, PRAYER MEANS "talking to God." I have defined prayer (in *Prayer on Wings*) as "conscious communication with the Deity." This definition makes room for both communication *to* God, often through words and communication *from* God, often through silence and images. In this book, I use the term *meditation* to refer to imagery prayer, because meditation often connotes the more intuitive nontalking forms of prayer.

Robert E. Ornstein offers a helpful classification of meditation types.[7] He distinguishes between *concentrative* and *opening-up*. In *concentrative* meditation, one seeks to let go of the chatter of thought that constantly occurs in the mind by focusing intensely and exclusively upon an object: sound (word, chant, sound in nature), physical movement (repetitive dance, routine gestures), visual object (symbol, picture, mandala), body function (breath), or combinations of these objects used simultaneously. After a period of such intense concentration, one is more alert to and aware of the fullness of life. One has practiced letting go of distractions, thereby strengthening the ability to attend, to concentrate. Through this practice, a person can develop the ability to give greater attention to a friend in conversation, to a musical recording or a book, to a problem needing solution, or even to God.

In *opening-up* meditation, one tries to be fully aware while participating in action. One might walk or jog, remaining attentive to the experience. Or one might draw or write, letting pictures or words flow uncensored.

Many meditations are combinations of these two types, as are those in this book. These are *concentrative* in that one lets go of other thoughts while focusing upon the given scene. The meditations are also *opening-up*, allowing a flow of personal images, thoughts, and feelings. We can consider these two functions as analogous to the view through a window. The given biblical passage and suggested scene provide the frame, the *concentrative* element. The personal visualization during the meditation is the view through the window, the *opening-up* element.

Imagery prayer is a holistic approach to prayer. When people talk to God using discourse prayer, images accompany their speech—they just are not particularly aware of those images. In congregational prayer when a person names a concern, giving the horrible details of the problem, the description evokes an image to some degree in the mind of the hearers—those who are about to pray. If a pastor prays for peace in some country on the earth, parishioners imagine something—intended or not—either warlike motifs or peaceful scenes. Yet persons perceive these images as separate from the prayer, as two different things.

By contrast, in imagery prayer, the images not only occur during the prayer itself but also are aligned with the goal of the prayer. Beyond the visual, imagery prayer often elicits tactile, auditory, and olfactory images. We involve more of our whole being in the prayer; more of us is potentially open. Of course discernment afterward is a necessary part of the entire process.

IMAGERY IN RELIGIOUS TRADITION

THE CONTENT OF THE BIBLE bears witness to the worldview, values, and images of the time that shaped the Bible—both orally and in its written form. Sometimes these values and images are implicit or hidden; other times they are explicit and obvious. The biblical world of wheat, tares, olives, mountains, fish, seas, fishermen, and treasures fill our minds as we read. Our images probably bear *some* resemblance to the actual life lived by those persons in the biblical narrative, but complete likeness is lacking. Even if we know something about fishing, searching for treasures, and growing olives, we literally cannot imagine something completely congruent with the lives really lived by Jesus, Esther, Paul, or an "unnamed woman" of the biblical narrative. If we have visited the Holy Land or seen the ancient tombs of Rome, we still cannot feel what it would have been like centuries ago.

Each of us also lives now with a worldview that is partially evident but to some degree implicit and unacknowledged. Our worldview varies according to whether we are a twenty-year-old Korean American collegiate math major living in Los Angeles, a forty-something African American public school teacher living in Dayton, or a retired Anglo American tobacco farmer living in Wheeling. Sometimes whether we are the collegiate, the public school teacher, or the tobacco farmer, we think that we are supposed to get into the biblical text, forgetting our own contexts. Yet we have no reason to do that, and we could not if we tried. It is both legitimate and inevitable that we bring our worlds to the biblical world as we read the Bible. We experience an interplay between the text and our present situation.[8]

This moving back and forth between ancient and contemporary worlds occurs when we read the Bible in an ordinary literary fashion. However, this interplay between the biblical worldview and our particular worldviews becomes more obvious when we enter into imagery meditation on scripture. On two occasions, one twenty years ago and one recently, I was with some Asian Christians as they practiced imagery meditation on scripture. At the first event, a gentleman from Japan apologized for not being able to see "wheat"; he knew only how rice grew. The Koreans with whom I prayed recently told me that they needed to study the Middle East geography and terrain more fully if they were to practice biblical imagery often. In both cases, the barrier was geographic—an inability to imagine the terrain described in the Judeo-Christian Bible. Yet it is a local terrain. Meditators have no reason to imagine wheat; it is fine to imagine rice. Olives, papayas, bananas, and snow peas are interchangeable in these prayers. Today we do not bury people in cave tombs. So seeing an "empty tomb" translates into very different meanings in our various cultures. Those who pray need to accept that they can translate the particulars however they need to.

The intentional evoking of biblical images through meditation is not new. Saint Ignatius taught guided imagery based on biblical passages in the Christian church four hundred years ago. He chose passages such as the Incarnation, Jesus at the temple, the Last Supper, the Passion, and the Resurrection for what he called "mental image" meditations. The following is Saint Ignatius's contemplation upon the Nativity. I quote it in its entirety to show the way in which he set the stage.

> *The first prelude* is to review the history of the Nativity. How our Lady, almost nine months with child, set out from Nazareth, seated on an ass, as may piously be believed, together with Joseph and a servant girl leading an ox. They are going to Bethlehem to pay the tribute that Caesar has imposed on the whole land.
>
> *The second prelude* is to form a mental image of the scene and see in my imagination the road from Nazareth to Bethlehem. I will consider its length and breadth, and whether it is level or winding through valleys and over hills. I will also behold the place of the cave of the Nativity, whether it is large or small, whether high or low, and what it contains.
>
> *The third prelude* will be the same and in the same form as it was in the preceding contemplation.

The first point is to see the persons: our Lady and St. Joseph, the servant girl, and the Child Jesus after his birth. I will become a poor, miserable, and unworthy slave looking upon them, contemplating them, and ministering to their needs, as though I were present there. I will then reflect within myself in order that I may derive some fruit.

The second point is to observe, consider, and contemplate what they are saying and to reflect within myself that I may derive some profit.

The third point is to observe and consider what they are doing: the journey and suffering which they undergo in order that our Lord might be born in extreme poverty, and after so many labors; after hunger and thirst, heat and cold, insults and injuries. He might die on the cross, and all this for me. I will then reflect in order to gain some spiritual profit.

The Colloquy. Conclude with a colloquy as in the preceding contemplation and with the "Our Father."[9]

Saint Ignatius suggested projectively moving into the biblical episode—being there, listening, watching, even conversing with the people within the scene. Yet clearly he did not use the imagination exercise solely to understand the biblical situation and its teachings. He expected personal growth too. Likewise, persons may expect both personal growth *and* increased understanding of the Bible as a result of practicing the meditations in this volume.

For those who would enjoy other resources for guided meditations, I suggest Mary Zimmer's *Sister Images: Guided Meditations from the Stories of Biblical Women.*

Leading Imagery Prayer

THE APPROACH I TAKE IN THIS BOOK differs from the Ignatian approach. I suggest that when engaging in dialogue with people in the biblical scene, you decide whether to let them into your setting in time or to enter into their setting in time. Similarly, you can stay close to the biblical words and content or let contemporary and personal meanings develop. Where Ignatius was bold in getting across his theology within the meditation, I attempt to allow maximum flexibility.

If you lead others in imagery prayer, it helps to distinguish among three types of visualization: receptive, programmed, or guided.[10] Receptive visualization is what occurs when a person closes her eyes and simply notices the images that appear. No scene whatsoever is suggested. The second type, programmed visualization, requires someone to tell the visualizer what to see. If a coach says, "See yourself in your mind crossing the finish line. See yourself. Imagine it," that coach is using programmed visualization. Conscious control over the images exists. The person tries to visualize the planned and suggested images. Many people employ programmed imagery for growth, healing, stress or pain reduction, or release from addiction.

The third type of visualization is guided, which combines receptive and programmed elements. These meditations employ this type of visualization. The written words will set the scene, letting those who visualize fill in the "blanks" with their own unconscious stirrings or conscious direction.

According to the purposes and personality of the leader, the degree of "programming" compared to "receptivity" varies. Some people program many suggestions, especially if they want the one(s) who follow them in the meditation to think or feel a certain way.

An example will illustrate different approaches. A woman who is now a minister sat in a covenant group years ago while the group prayed. She could not follow the group's praying because her mind kept imagining the operating room in which her father was having surgery at that exact moment. She "saw" the doctors and nurses leaning over her father. The doctor asked the nurse for a scalpel. When he reached out his hand to receive the tool, the meditator noticed the "marks of the cross" on his hands. The doctor's own hands were bleeding, as Christ's hands. This image comforted the meditator, reassuring her that Christ was present at the surgery. Since that time, this woman has told others who were anticipating surgery of her experience. She has suggested that they look for some sign of Christ's presence as they imagined their own or another's surgery. One person, she recalls, observed the smiles of the nurses as such a sign.

A minister prompts these spontaneous images, but the images are unique to the ones who pray. I would not suggest to others that they imagine the presence of Christ by visualizing a doctor with the wounded hands of Christ. That image may be intrusive or even frightening. Moreover, it would not be their image. A good deal of the efficacy of imagery is the personal synthesis that takes place. We rob persons of that opportunity when we impose our integrations.

My own solution to this dilemma is to set the scene as sparsely as possible and to offer many options. I suggest, for example, that one realize that the Christ is present, but I leave it to the meditators to decide how. I give choices as to whether and how to interact, not even indicating that dialogue or speech takes place, in case nonverbal interaction is called for.

THE USE OF IMAGERY IN RELIGIOUS EDUCATION, SPIRITUAL DIRECTION, PASTORAL CARE

CHILDREN CLEARLY USE THEIR IMAGINATIONS spontaneously, and parents encourage this use by perpetuating belief in Santa Claus, tooth fairies, and the acceptance of imaginary friends at the dinner table. Adults do imagine; in fact we applaud imaginatively gifted adults. But for the most part, adults do not actively cultivate or continue to educate themselves in the domain of imagination.

These guided meditations are primarily for adults and teenagers. They provide a way to help the young maintain their active imaginations and to help adults repossess theirs. Activities abound that help educate people of any age to use their imaginations. Use *your* imagination to create some.[11]

As a Sunday school teacher of fourth through sixth graders, I was to teach the class about the sacrament of baptism. Sacraments, grace, and the symbolic meanings of water can get rather abstract for adults, let alone older elementary children. So we used our imaginations to recall experiences with water. We sat on both sides of a long table, which was covered with paper. After dimming the lights and becoming quiet, we each recalled a time when we had fun with water (in any of its states), drawing images of those times. We recalled a time when we desperately needed water, then drew those images. Finally, we each recollected a time when water scared us, and we drew those images. While remembering and drawing, we concentrated by being silent, as silent as ten to twelve year olds can be.

Afterward, we talked about the experiences with water that we had depicted. Vividly, children recalled needing water when they were sick, after playing baseball and basketball, when cleaning off from a beach trip, and to put out a fire. They were scared of water in storms, when falling into deep ponds, and when hot water caused a burn. They had fun with water in swimming pools, when ice-covered driveways allowed for ice hockey or ice skating at home, and watching the sunshine reflect on a lake.

After such an enjoyable experience imagining water, the children used their imaginations again while studying the sacrament of Communion. Trying to get into the mind-set of Jesus at the Last Supper, we recalled a meal we remembered because of the people we were with or because of the food we ate. We recalled a memorable meal at a holiday and a meal that was a "last time" for something. Again we shared the events—from the first time trying ham at a relative's home to the "last" hot pretzel at a Dayton Dynamos' soccer game before the team moved to Cincinnati.

Pastoral caregiving and spiritual direction wisely includes the intentional use of imagery. When a couple is repeating an argument or rehashing a similar theme, the minister can request that they shift to imagination. The clergyperson asks each to visualize the other as an image or symbol, taking time to allow an image to settle. Then the clergy asks each to include himself or herself in that same image. Afterward, they share the symbols or images held of the other and of themselves when included in the scene.

An illustration makes this exercise clear: A woman imagines her husband as a trapeze artist, taking risky, yet beautiful dives in front of admiring, applauding audiences. When she places herself in the image, she stands by the net, hoping he does not fall. The man imagines his wife painting the outside of their house independent in her decisions and able to climb ladders to achieve her goal alone. When he puts himself into the scene, he is the mail deliverer, noticing her progress daily. As they hear each other's symbolic sketches, they laugh, yet see how the scenes reveal truths about their relationship. Each experiences himself or herself as "watching" or "waiting on" the other. They would like to be more interdependent; they would like to matter more to each other.

Using the imagination suggests that the couple has resources they can use to help themselves. The clergyperson does not tell them what to do in their behavior as a couple but rather offers a way for them to reflect. Often the use of the imagination breaks through repetitious "logical" arguments. Finally the imagination offers different ground on which to talk.[12]

Self-disciplined individuals may record their dreams and seek imagery prayer on their own or after someone—an educator, clergy, spiritual director, preacher—makes clear the benefits. Ministers and educators may accept persons' sharing of images and dreams as part of normal discourse. (Setting aside special "counseling" sessions is valuable. But some brief discussions of images can take place casually, just as parishioners talk about their extended family members' health, expecting some response.)

A woman who takes much interest in her dreams and images (who is also an ardent activist for people in need) casually commented when we met on a sidewalk that she had a dream in which she "climbed *into* prison"! That dream validated her decision to step out of a painful working relationship. She did not need or seek out counseling but did appreciate the chance to name her insight, to have it heard.

I experienced a similar phenomenon while serving a congregation. People started to take their images and dreams seriously, informing the minister about them, just as they informed clergy about their social concerns for the neighborhood or about their children's soccer games. Richness of experience, guidance, and a deepened relationship can develop without the expenditure of much time with this casual openness to the sharing of images. However, certain individuals may present an image or dream, raising the question, "So, what does it mean?" I have learned to refuse to answer such a question "on the run." If persons are not going to do their own reflection first, I require a counseling session to work with them. Persons need to put forth effort to take their images seriously rather than expecting others to tell them what their images mean.

Most experiences with imagery are positive and satisfying, even when they seem to challenge the one who prays. On rare occasions, persons have difficulty because what they imagine puts them into a predicament. If they are part of a group, they may not get the help they need to resolve the problem quickly.

A young woman who participated for a while in the congregation I served in San Diego told me she could no longer practice imagery meditation, because she had a "bad experience." After talking briefly, I asked whether she would like to try to bring some closure to the prior experience, and she agreed. When we met, she explained that the leader had guided her (through imagination) into a dark room. Somehow she was to get out of the room, but in her own imagination she never exited. She remained—in her imagination—frightened and stranded in the room.

I explained to her that she was in charge of her own images; she could invent or find something that would help her. She could ask for assistance in the imagery experience itself. She relaxed and closed her eyes. I suggested that she move back into that dark room, if she felt she could calmly. She explored the room, feeling around until she found a match, which she struck. That gave her enough light to find the exit door.

This illustrates three dilemmas that do occur in imagery when practiced in a group. First, she needed a reminder to ask for assistance. Then she needed closure, time and guidance to proceed through her images toward satisfaction. Finally, she needed to reflect upon connections between this imagery predicament and that of her own waking life. She pondered, *Do I reach closure, ask for assistance, experience "darkness" or feel as if I'm in the dark, find "striking" solutions, feel alone or trapped, or need to "get out" of anything in my waking life?*

When we work with an individual alone, that person can talk aloud as he or she images, enabling us to move cautiously and encouragingly in the direction that the person is taking.[13] Group imagery does not allow for this care. For that reason, avoid "darkness" or anything potentially scary with groups.

One may enlist imagination in other meaningful ways to provide care and nurture. For the anniversary of a marriage, the founding of a church, or the death of a loved one, we can enlist imagery to gather up precious memories. We can do this even in worship. For example, my pastor asked the members of the congregation to recollect scenes from the life of Dietrich Bonhoeffer on the Sunday that marked fifty years since Bonhoeffer's death in a concentration camp. He slowly pictured biographic events, not telling us to imagine them, but describing these events clearly, in such a style that our imaginations would have to be numb not to respond.

When a couple celebrates an anniversary, they can "walk backward in their minds" to let joyous, funny, difficult, lovely experiences bathe them.[14] When a girl enters puberty or a boy shaves for the first time, the youth and their family members can imaginatively "relive" some important steps in their lives thus far, treasuring every new stage, while giving thanks for the newest one.

MEANINGS OF IMAGES AND SYMBOLS: PERSONAL AND COLLECTIVE

MANY PSYCHOLOGICAL APPROACHES AGREE with the premise that symbols can be unique to an individual and at the same time have some general, universal meaning. The Gestalt therapy approach to dream and imagery symbolism stresses the unique meaning of the symbol. For example, in my twenties I had dozens of dreams in which I was exiting various kinds of "stalls." My "maiden" name was "Stahl," and I desired

27

both to leave that name and to marry. For others who did not have that association, exiting stalls would mean something entirely different!

Carl Jung, who explored the huge reservoir of archetypal symbols, still encouraged individuals to find idiosyncratic meanings for their own images. Joseph Campbell, known for his study of myths and symbols from many cultures, commented that change occurs so rapidly that myths become more and more personal. We tend to find our myths "as we go." Yet our own personal symbolism, as it emerges in dreams or images, still often expresses the same themes found in the myths of many cultures.

Psychosynthesis, an approach to therapy, frequently uses guided imagery in its group and individual work. It bases the imagery settings upon general wisdom regarding symbols while appreciating the uniqueness of personal symbolization. Even Artemidorus, in the second century C.E., pointed out that dream symbols have different meanings in different situations and for different persons.[15]

It seems abundantly clear that people respond differently to a symbol and bring to it a wide variety of meanings. The same symbol may evoke several different meanings for the same individual over a period of time.

In the meditations, I refer to Jesus as "the Christ." Since a symbol evokes more than the picture of the object referred to, "the Christ" is more clearly a symbol than "Jesus." "The Christ" evokes something beyond the historical person, although it includes that. Persons may visualize "the Christ" in many ways: male, female, star-like, as a voice, or as a collective group of those who carry on the work and presence of Jesus.[16] Recall that the one who prayed for her loved one in surgery experienced Christ as present in her imagery because of the wounds on the surgeon's hands.

The following chart lists some common symbols and their frequently evoked meanings. These connections help explain the choice of scenes in a number of the meditations in this book. Also this list can guide you in creating your own imagery prayers. Remember that these are to some extent culture bound and that they also reflect personal idiosyncrasies. Some people have never seen a meadow; perhaps a cement-and-flower-potted city square, a calm high desert, or a dusty outback field would work as contextual equivalents. Individuals who do not feel that they have "green thumbs" may have difficulties with the imagery related to planting seeds. Yet other experiences may evoke images of growth—yeast while baking, crescendos in music, competency in some activity.

Symbol	Often Evokes
Meadow (grassy area)	a neutral situation or present consciousness
Sun	a center (for action, balance, and source) a form of energy (for growth, warmth) a form of order, regularity eternal life disengaged from time
Wise person	wisdom, for guidance sense of call from the Divine, the part of the self which is able to transcend the self

The *meadow*, *sun*, and *wise person* are the "safest," most nurturing symbols to use.

Plant (flower, seed)	an aspect of growth
Water (pool, beach, river)	an aspect of feeling flow of energy (river) the unconscious
Forest	the unconscious that is near to the surface

Caves (going down)	the lower, deeper unconscious
Mountain (going up)	the higher, superconscious, or transpersonal dimension of self
Gift	facilitates "grounding," bridging the image experience to daily life (See chapter 3, debriefing and grounding)
House (dwelling)	view of the personality, or how one sees oneself, perhaps with the rooms as different aspects of the self

During a guided meditation in October 1975, a *dandelion* emerged as a symbol of the qualities that I sought to embody. Dandelions are not planted; they simply pop up. They are carefree of the judgments of others—free to wander, to squeeze in solo fashion between other flowers or together, to proliferate, dominating an entire field for a few weeks in spring.

At that time, living in southern California rather than in Dayton, Ohio, I actually was less acquainted with dandelions. But I needed inner resilience from the judgment or comments of others as well as from my own internal "oughts." I used the image of a dandelion for almost a year while praying, gradually incorporating the qualities that it represented to me then.

You may have symbols that frequent your meditations or you may rarely notice the same image. Avoid attachment to a particular symbol; be willing to release it when you no longer need it. If you do not recognize recurring images, deliberately keep a journal of your dream or prayer images. Probably the recurring themes or symbols will surprise you.

GUIDED IMAGERY IN PUBLIC WORSHIP

I REFER TO THESE EXERCISES as meditations or prayer, because I believe that they are "conscious communication with the Deity." Some clergy may try to use these as a basis for a sermon or instead of a sermon. When I attempted this use with the congregation I served, a rather vocal group felt cheated. They thought I had avoided preaching. This experience and a few others lead me to suggest that you use imagery prayer as only part of the sermon or as another portion of the worship rather than the sermon.

A second reason for not using imagery prayer as a substitute for a sermon is that some persons do not like imagery prayer. They either refuse to do it or insist that they cannot image. This resistance to imagery prayer lessens when it serves as another part of the liturgy.

Another consideration leads toward not substituting an imagery prayer for a sermon. It is tempting for the pastor to preach through the imagery prayer, which is an inappropriate use of this medium. Either we are proclaiming the gospel as we grasp it, or we are asking congregants to be receptive to the stirrings of the Spirit themselves as they pray. Pastors should not tell congregants what stirrings are going on in their minds.

Even if we do not intentionally preach, what occurs at the "sermon time" tends to take on a different feel to the listener. For many, this time has more authority. One woman who told me that she did not like imagery prayer explained, "I don't like people telling me what to do. I'm independent." This woman did not mind sermons. I think that what she did not like was someone's telling her what to do under the pretense that she herself, in her own mind, was in charge. She was astute in her grasp of the problem.

After stating these precautions, I acknowledge that for some congregations and some ministers, an imagery prayer as a sermon works. Bravo.

For virtually every other portion of the liturgy, the use of guided imagery prayer can spark interest and develop an appreciation for novelty. One key is to use imagery sparingly. Offer this type of prayer sufficiently often that visualization becomes familiar, but not so frequently that it becomes mundane.

Index IV lists the meditations and their various uses within the liturgy: "Call to Worship," "Invocation," "Prayer of Confession," "Offertory," "Benediction," and other portions of the liturgy. The index also suggests meditations for particular celebrations, such as baptism, Communion, or the recognition of teachers.

2

Understanding Guidance from God

GOD IS INCARNATE, as present to the imagination as the reasoning capacity, as present to the will as the physical body, the aesthetic sensitivity, the five senses, intuition, or the emotions. God presents bountiful guidance through each of these avenues all the time. God intervenes every second, if we but see, imagine, will, taste, think, or feel those interventions.

Sometimes large "revelations" appear—times when divine guidance bursts forth, or we humans grasp God's will in some especially congruent way. Most of the time, revelation is consistent, persistent, and plentiful but not necessarily easy to discern.

Protestant Christianity has affirmed four sources for divine revelation: scripture, tradition, reason, and experience. Naming these avenues for God's revelation is useful, but only if we realize that the four are not separate entities. Consider scripture. Tradition, reason, and experience are integral to scripture itself. Jesus was a rabbi of the Hebrew *tradition*; he spoke of it often. The *experiences* of Lazarus, Joanna, Zipporah, and Mordecai are integral to their faith. Again and again the people of scripture (and in some ancient stories, even God) *reason* what they should do. Scripture presents Noah, David, Tamar, and Elizabeth as *reasoning* amidst their life experiences.

Consider experience. Both tradition and scripture greatly influence experience for many. A woman *experiences* a call to ministry. The possibility of her ordination depends upon the *tradition* within Christianity to which she belongs. While experience can transform, usually it translates into action only when linked to *reason*. Scripture records Paul's struggle to integrate his rational belief with his experience of transformation.

I immensely enjoyed being at a Lakota Sioux campfire amidst drumming, singing, and dancing. My *experience* tells me that it was a sacred time with my daughter, dancing with Native Americans at the Rosebud Reservation. Since that time I call upon *reason* to reflect on the Lakota thought-world and my Anglo-Christian worldview.

Consider tradition. Tradition by itself is a horrible basis for decision making. If one does what grandma did only because she did it, without knowing her situation or thinking about one's own circumstances, one would be ignoring several decades of change. These changes affect the meaning of the tradition. ("Why do you use such a large pot to cook potatoes?" inquired the son of the mother. "Because Grandma always did." "Grandma, why did you use such a big pot?" the son persists. Answers Grandma, "Because I didn't have a small one.") Tradition is a source of guidance when combined with reason and experiential wisdom; tradition without reason and experience is hollow.

Revelation occurs through all the aspects of our bodily being, through the variety of cultural aspects, and through nature itself. We should consult as many avenues as possible, as often as possible. Because we often do not bring into play our imagination, we should. Let us look more closely at the "Protestant Quadrilateral" (scripture, tradition, reason, and experience) as those sources specifically relate to imagery prayer.

SCRIPTURE

PEOPLE USE AND UNDERSTAND the Judeo-Christian scriptures as an avenue of God's revelation in many ways. My view is that no particular book, time, or context can completely contain divine revelation. I believe revelation takes place in relation—the relation between the human's opening up and the Divine's revealing[1] and also among all created beings. In imagery meditation on scripture, the goal is not to find a message deep within the words or worldview of the passage but to be in relationship with the Divine. The passage, given its poignancy in the life of ancient Jews and early Christians, its potency for centuries of Christians and Jews, and its relevance for you can enable you to experience the sacred in your own time through your thoughts and images. Ruth and Jacob are more likely to come to your mind with sacred impact than an imaginary Juan or Kalila, drawn from a contemporary novel. Yet you are free to bring into meditation characters from your contemporary world of images, if they enhance your inner dialogue.

One approach to biblical study is to focus on telling the stories of the Hebrew Scriptures and New Testament. In fact, the "Network of Biblical Storytellers"[2] meets to foster the telling of Bible stories, often from memory. Thomas Boomershine, the network's founder, reminds us that the Gospels originally were spoken. They are part of Israel's great storytelling tradition.

If we know, really know, a biblical story by "heart," it can affect us deeply. In time of need we bring it to mind—to heart. It has healing efficacy. Some people enjoy and benefit from hearing a biblical story, not just in worship but by their bedside.

The telling of the biblical stories and guided imagery on scripture have several parallels. Both are experiential. Both approaches assume that the biblical stories are such that one can "enter" them, have a relationship with them. In each practice, the experience itself is often significant, though persons derive additional insight from reflections afterward.

Walter Wink, Conrad E. L'Heureux, and other biblical scholars recommend involvement with the biblical texts by acting them out or engaging in some form of dialogue, often with others in a small group.[3] It is certainly possible to act out many of the meditations in this volume.

TRADITION

IMAGINATION IS BOTH CREATION and discovery. It seems to us that we construct our images; but at the same time, the images appear to "come to us." Actually, our imagination is embedded in a variety of traditions that mediate our world to us. Our past profoundly influences us in ways we cannot imagine.

Living in the Western Christian tradition, the mention of "Adam and Eve," "Mary and Martha," or "King David" evokes reactions for us. The images generated by the names are not neutral. Sometimes the Judeo-Christian tradition influences people who consider themselves post-Christian as much as it influences those who consider themselves Christian, for what one has chosen to go "beyond" still has meaning.

Bishop John A. T. Robinson reminded us in his 1963 book *Honest to God* that some who do not believe in God are more attached to particular notions of God (which they don't believe in) than those who do believe. They need the assurance that God is an unbelievable being, so they can continue not to believe.

Realizing the effect of tradition upon us is very helpful when we practice guided meditations. Sometimes the image's prior meanings can be helpful. Other times we need to divest a particular passage or character of irrelevant meanings to gain novel and creative insight. For this reason, some discussion of the biblical passages (or personal reflection, if you practice alone) is an essential part of the process. We need to get ready to meditate. Part of the opening process is the cleansing away of old meanings.

The meditations with Martha and Mary usually bring a good deal of response in contemporary women precisely because "tradition" has encrusted those two with such stereotypes. Although the scripture never mentions Martha's cooking, sermons have depicted her so vividly that, to the imagination of many, she cooks. By reading the Gospel accounts of Martha and Mary carefully and by using fresh imagination in meditation, one can scrutinize the tradition of Martha—accepting it as tradition has handed it down or changing it in one's own experience.

Together, imagination and tradition can be a marvelous and powerful duo. Tradition reminds us of past ways, chosen for some reason that perhaps we should not forget. Imagination reminds us of future options, available for reasons that perhaps we should not ignore.

REASON

IT IS IMPORTANT THAT IMAGES ALONE not be taken as direct guidance from God. Do not act on something you imagine—especially from one meditation—unless you reflect rationally and think through the decision or action with another. Images have many symbolic as well as literal meanings; you need to consider the symbolic meanings too.

You may image that you marry a particular individual. Do not go marry or ask to marry that person; especially do not persuade the potential spouse by saying that God guided you to marry or to ask! Symbolically, to "marry" can mean many things. For example, it could point toward the incorporation of some important qualities of that other into your life. It could serve as a reminder that marriage is ever-present to your mind, that you should let go of your preoccupation. Or a "marrying" scene in visualization may be a pun—don't let all the crises in your life get you down, be "merry."

Also, images not only present what we should do but often what we *want* to do, even if we *shouldn't*. It is our responsibility to discern the difference, using whatever help we can locate. Chapter 3 includes a variety of suggestions for grounding and debriefing, an essential step of rational reflection.

Reason bears upon our meditating in another significant way. We have rational understandings about how the universe is put together, how it functions. If we assume that the world is like a machine with parts, we may assume that outside forces care for and drive the parts. God is out there, for example. Then we continue to create that machine-like reality, to some extent, in our imagination and in our daily living. We consider ourselves and others as cogs in wheels or bytes in computers. By contrast, if we assume that the world is an organism with related and interdependent aspects, we may assume that the power that connects the various parts is also taking care of the whole. Then we continue to create that organic-like reality, to some extent, in our imagination and in our daily living. We consider ourselves and others as fingers, toes, blood, and bile—all different, yet reciprocally essential for life.[4]

We receive our worldviews from our traditions—both religious and secular. Several worldviews influenced the telling and recording of our scriptures. Rational thinking through the past centuries has elevated the mechanistic image; however, the organic image is more compatible with large portions of our biblical heritage. We need both imagination and reason to consider and foster healthy worldviews.

EXPERIENCE

PRACTICING THESE MEDITATIONS is certainly "experiential Bible study."

However, experience is not cut off from other avenues of revelation but integrally related to them.

John Biersdorf notes five qualities that distinguish *experience*:
1. Experience connects inner and outer reality.
2. Experience is worthwhile not solely as a means to some end but in and of itself.
3. Experience is sensed to be connected with meaning.
4. Important experience challenges one's view of reality; one must take this new event into account.
5. Experience may be spontaneous *or* may be intentionally planned and sought after.[5]

Each of these experiential qualities bears directly upon the use of the meditations in this book. Simply practicing them, regardless of later reflections or actions, is worthwhile. Like a dream we do not recall, the imagery functions to sort through anxieties and hopes at an unconscious level.

Yet more than in most prayer forms, we actually do find guidance within the imagery meditation. We discover that we do have hope, that we are feeling barren, that we cannot yet forgive, that we are grateful for relationships, or that we should work on our judgmental nature. We piece together the abundant clues so they make sense to us.

You may find it useful to keep track of images by recording them in a journal. Watching them over a period of time usually reveals some meaning. But it is fine to live with the sense that something has meaning that we cannot—and never will—clearly understand. This experience is similar to witnessing a sunset. We seldom claim a discernible meaning, but the experience has meaning nevertheless.

Prayer that intentionally includes images can help us feel events in our lives in a new way. Consider a man who is six months from retirement. Without his prior knowledge, the company hires a person to assist him in his work. At first the man feels rejected and betrayed, as if he is being ridiculed to need help. He is livid. Then, as he stays with his work, he begins to enjoy teaching the new worker, passing on his knowledge and skills. By the time of his actual retirement, he appreciates having been able to train his successor.

These changes in feelings from rejection and betrayal to anger, and finally to enjoyment and gratitude occurred naturally over time, even without specific prayer related to this concern. However, for some, conditions get worse. Not everyone naturally heals, given their histories and their current situations. Imagery prayer can function as a booster shot for those with healthy dispositions and supportive, nurturing environments. But it can be a breakthrough for those with less encouraging domains. I have not known a person to practice imagery prayer and become more distraught over the long haul. Some may awaken to feelings they had denied (and that is uncomfortable), but that very awareness tends to lead toward healing. I am convinced that the meditations' scriptural base helps people to believe and to expect a healing of emotions.

MOVING BEYOND OUR OWN PERSPECTIVES

ONE OF THE IMPERATIVES of Christianity—taught over and over by Jesus—is to take another perspective. One has to learn and to cultivate this ability to move beyond one's own immediate experience, to "transcend" oneself.

Developmental psychologists theorize that children must reach a certain age (perhaps seven) before they are actually capable of differentiating their own point of view from another's. A parent or teacher may say, "Darrell, consider how doing that makes LaTanya feel." Or a sitter yells, "Susie, think how I feel!" This is good training. Eventually Darrell, LaTanya, and Susie will be able to consider how another feels. But until the ability to think abstractly develops, it is not actually possible.

Many adults have minimal capacity to walk in another's shoes. That is precisely the reason Jesus told parables that pushed us to consider the worker who waited all day for a job, the widow who contributed her tiny income, or the lilies of the fields. He tried to get his friends and followers to "transcend" themselves.

The meditations in this book definitely can help us "see" from another perspective within the limits of our own imagination—and God's persuasive power. We can practice "Extending Our Families" (Number 48), first seeing through the eyes of the beloved disciple, then through the eyes of Mary, then from Jesus' perspective. Or we can imagine what it would be like to be foreign, to be desperate, and to face insult just to have the chance for our daughter's healing ("Holy, Humble, Indefatigable, and Healed," Meditation 32). We can empathize with the woman at the well as she gradually realizes with whom she is talking ("Being Known and Knowing Christ," Meditation 13).

While discussing empathy with a group of pastors, I read aloud the so-called "children's" book *The True Story of the Three Little Pigs* by Jon Scieszka. The wolf tells the story from his perspective—a rather different version than the one told by the pigs. One pastor's further study of empathy inspired him to preach a sermon on the story of David and Goliath—from the perspective of Goliath! His message gave the congregation permission and encouragement to take another perspective, to realize that everything we are told *has* a perspective.

We are called to break down stereotypes and prejudices. Seeing another side, another angle, outside the box, helps us to do that. Otherwise, we're stuck. Imagination is a gift that can enable this moral, social transformation.

3

Guidelines for Using These Meditations

PREPARING ONESELF OR A GROUP

The Body

Each of the meditations begins with instructions to relax. Most of the time I suggest taking several deep breaths. Sometimes I recommend the movement of parts of the body, the tensing and relaxing of body sections, or getting a sense of one's location.

Whether alone or in a group, give attention to your physical condition and location before starting the imagery prayer. This allows you to focus, to reduce distractions, and to gather your will toward the meditation. Please use whatever relaxes and calms you, regardless of the suggestions at the beginning of the meditation you choose.

Posture is important. An upright posture, with head above the spine, maximizes your ability to stay alert and minimizes distractions from the body. Sitting straight in a chair or sitting cross-legged on the floor is fine. Some persons recline to practice imagery meditation; however, it is easy to fall asleep in that position.

Meditation does affect the body. Studies on the effects of repeating a phrase again and again demonstrate that one's oxygen consumption, respiratory rate, heart rate, blood pressure, and muscle tension tend to decrease, and alpha waves increase while meditating.[1] Given the hurriedness of our present culture, these physical effects are probably healthy for us.

Beginning Guided Prayer

If you are meditating alone, read the passage, the BIBLICAL NOTE, and the FOR YOUR MEDITATION sections first. Then read through the meditation several times, close your eyes, and practice the meditation according to your memory. It does not need to be precise.

Or read the meditation into a tape recorder (or videotape), playing it back for yourself. If you choose this approach, read slowly. When meditating, you can turn the machine off and on, giving yourself whatever time you need before the next spoken words.

Another method involves reading a small section of the meditation, then closing your eyes to meditate upon that portion. Open your eyes to read the next portion; close your eyes to meditate, and so on.

If you lead a group in the practice of these meditations, start by reading the biblical passage. Take time to discuss the passage. Tell others your insights, but also hear group members' reactions, memories, and understandings about the passage. The more thoroughly persons discuss the biblical passage, the more investment they have in their meditation. The scene has come to mean more to them. Interestingly, people seem freer to let go of the precise scriptural details in their prayer once they have talked about them.

Practicing these meditations during worship requires little fanfare. Simply say, "I'd like you to close your eyes and join me in a guided meditation."

I encourage you to adapt these meditations for your purpose and setting. Explore in order to find what works best for you. You can create your own meditations based on other scripture passages. I once asked people to imagine loving God "with all your heart, with all your soul, with all your mind, and with all your strength" (Mark 12:30). I thought that it would evoke a sense of wholeness. However, a number of people were frustrated. The image suggestions were not sufficiently concrete. Consider the difference when asked to visualize finding a buried treasure. The treasure is quite precise and concrete; loving God "with all one's soul" is not. The more visual the imagery in the biblical scene itself, the more likely it is to be a productive meditation.

Safety Factors and Dangers

Because all of one's psyche is available for every meditation, something out of the distant past or the deeper unconscious—something strange, confrontational, or threatening—could emerge with any meditation. However, some scenes lend themselves better to calm nurturance than others. This book includes "safer" passages: symbols and settings that generally evoke nurturing, nonthreatening, present or future-oriented images rather than confrontational or distant-past-oriented experiences.

In the first edition, I did not include a meditation that surrounded Jesus on the cross. In the revised edition, I have included one with Jesus talking to his mother and his Beloved Disciple ("Extending Our Families") and one on the Resurrection ("Christ Has Risen!—An Empty Tomb"). Over the past two decades I have come to worry less about the dangers of imagery meditation because so many people find that visualizing even difficult situations produces insight and even comfort.

However, I would never suggest that people imagine Jesus' actual crucifixion or focus on violence or death. In some therapy situations with individuals, one might pursue such suggestions with the individual's telling the therapist aloud what is occurring during the meditation. But that use is beyond the expectations of this book.

The meditation "Preparing a Place for Us: Saying Good-bye" may lead to expressions of grief, anger, or loneliness. Be aware of this and use it with discretion. The leader is more obliged to provide time for debriefing when using passages that might evoke deep feeling. People will need to recount their experiences and be heard.

Some visualization books and resources suggest that persons imagine entering a cave or going down into a basement. This symbolism tends to evoke memories or images that are seldom made conscious by the meditator. I recommend that the leader avoid the suggestion of such symbols because of the potential emergence of repressed memories, which the meditator or group leader may be unprepared to handle. If meditators descend into basements while exploring their houses in "Let Your Light Shine," for example, fine—that is their choice. They may be particularly open to exploring those inner depths.

Aside from the safety factors in the choice of symbols and scenes for meditation, we each have a safety factor within. We have a beautiful regulating system that protects us from the conscious awareness of that which we are not yet ready to face. If we do not want an insight, we are likely to fall asleep, forget, or fail to see the connections in what our imagery is showing us.

Grief, anger, love, guilt, compassion, sadness, and joy can emerge if the meditator is willing to experience these emotions. The decision to face the many facets of our humanness is a significant one. I think that facing and confronting threatening images is important for psychological and spiritual maturation. We do not need to be overly cautious with meditation. However, it is wise to remind ourselves and others of our resources and strengths before seeking deliberately to open up the more vulnerable dimensions.

As a leader, state that you are available to discuss any concerns people have with visualization or with a particular meditation or image. Occasionally people need encouragement to bring closure to a meditation. For yourself or others, it is wise to find a professional therapist, spiritual director, or experienced pastor if further work is needed.

If you do not know the people whom you are leading in visualization, be particularly careful about the scenes or symbols used.

Timing

Those who lead a group in these meditations may discover that the whole process takes longer than expected. I once planned to use "The Vine-dresser, the Vine, and the Vineyard" as an opening prayer for a two-hour meeting. Those present became so involved that the meditation, along with the debriefing, took one and one-half hours. With a good deal of planning and intention, persons can practice imagery more swiftly. A five-hundred member congregation practiced a meditation on the Resurrection in five minutes.

If you have a time limit, rehearse the meditation itself to be sure how long it will take. Expand or contract the words. It is better to delete content than to rush the meditation. Allow time for meditators to develop images so that they are not frustrated that they don't have time to get a clear image before you move on to another scene.

Likewise, the individual meditator needs either to allow enough time or limit the meditation itself. Some persons set a timer in the next room to relieve them of the worry about the length of time they are taking.

Participants in groups often comment, "I needed more time. You went too fast." Others, but usually not as many, say the words came too slowly. Allow sufficient silence at the pauses, which are indicated by ellipses. While leading a meditation, I practice the meditation myself, so that I have my own pacing to follow. Alone or in a group, allow time at the end of the meditation to sit in silence. Some people will be completing their images.

Cultural and Personal Sensitivity

I have mentioned in the previous chapters that symbols are contextual. Some people are familiar with the biblical terrain, so sand, lakes, mountains, fishing, olives, even treasures make a good deal of sense. Others of us have lived in a very different environment: Alps, islands, fir trees, and swamps may populate our image world. Be as attentive to these differences as possible—naming them before the meditation, having choices within the meditation, and making room for diverse responses afterward.

Even people who share the same culture have personal idiosyncrasies that affect the meditation. We cannot anticipate all these uniquenesses, but be aware that people will react in various ways. Assure persons that they can change the given directions while meditating, or they can simply quit, sitting silently while the others meditate. Talk with them afterward to hear their suggestions for preparing the meditation in a better fashion in the future.

The following guidelines are to be read alone or presented to a group *prior* to the meditation whenever feasible. If a group practices regularly, the members would be wise to refresh their memories of these occasionally.

Since a listing of all these would be cumbersome within a worship setting, I suggest mentioning one or two each time visualization is used. In this way, the participants gradually hear them all. Repeat them as reminders thereafter.

EIGHT GUIDELINES

1. On "seeing"

While some "see" when they practice imagery prayer, most simply "get a sense" of the scene without a clear picture. Even people who say that they "see" do not see as clearly as if a movie screen were on the underside of their eyelids. Some practitioners are attentive to sounds, fragrances, and even tactile sensations.

2. On practice

Practice in using visualization definitely improves the ability and quality of the images or sensations.

3. On obeying

Do not feel you must "obey" the guiding words. If the image of putting on a clown face appears when the words of the meditation suggest that you plant a seed, decide whether to stay with your original clown image or to see if you can imagine planting a seed.

4. On "nothing" happening

If you think that nothing is happening, check out what that "nothing" is. You may be seeing one color only, experiencing a sense of joy, finding yourself upset about a person or situation, or daydreaming about things to do or a wonderful environment. Acknowledging what you consider to be "nothing" can bring insight, or it can help you refocus so that you can proceed with the meditation itself.

5. On asking for assistance

Bring in assistance or guidance by imagining a friend or "wise" person joining you in the scene. Or equip yourself: with a flashlight if the scene is dark, breathing gear if you are underwater; provide yourself with track shoes, crash helmet, food or drink whenever you want these. Since the scene is your creation, feel free to provide yourself with whatever you need.

6. On attachment

It is tempting to hold onto positive images a long time because they can be so nourishing. Likewise, "negative" images can worry us long after their brief significance served its purpose. Do not stay attached to the images. Make room for new ones when prior ones have served their purposes.

7. On debriefing and grounding

Debrief afterwards. Try to find some way to allow for personal reflection or interpersonal sharing. Facilitate grounding: Make images into concrete drawings, journal entries, or interesting crafts.

8. On succeeding

Do not worry about whether you've succeeded to practice properly! Just be open to visualize and see what happens.

DURING MEDITATION: FREQUENT PHENOMENA

These phenomena occur during guided visualization:

Falling asleep

A person may *fall asleep*, generally awakening at the end of the meditation. Or a person may hear part of the meditation's words and simply have no recall of the other parts. This occurs for several reasons:

- Some persons suddenly relax and, having previously formed the habit of falling asleep whenever they relax, they fall asleep. The path between the conscious and the unconscious becomes more accessible the more persons traverse it either through dream recall or imagery work.
- Some may not have gotten enough sleep!
- Some may already have enough on their minds so that they do not need or want any more input. (Perhaps they are investing a lot of energy in a crisis or creative project.)
- Some may be unwilling to face the topic or material that is emerging or could emerge right now in their lives. For example, they may be unwilling to acknowledge love for someone because that does not fit into their self-image, or they may not be ready to grieve a loss.
- Some may resist the leader or something about the situation.

If we fall asleep often during guided meditation, it is worthwhile to inquire why.

Going ahead of the meditation

A person may experience *going ahead of the meditation*; that is, doing in one's imagery what the verbal or written instructions have not yet suggested. This experience is not uncommon. In some cases it may occur due to the person's familiarity with the passage.

Picturing scenes from the past or imagining new scenes

A person may see *scenes from* his or her *past* when asked to see a meadow, seashore, or mountain. Another person may imagine *scenes* he or she has *never seen.*

Encountering Jesus and Mary

Encountering Jesus and Mary brings *mixed responses.* Some people are unable to talk to these biblical people during their imagery. Others have sexual fantasies. Some suddenly become concerned about how they themselves appear. What is important is to recognize what happens in the imagery and then to reflect upon how that does or does not relate to one's conscious life.

Resisting a return to the wakeful state

Some people say they *did not want to return to the wakeful state.* The leader wisely acknowledges this desire and suggests that the person reflect upon the reason for wanting to stay within the particular meditative scene. It is important that people return to the wakeful state after each meditation. Of course an individual can meditate again, enjoying or bringing to closure an earlier meditation.

Sharing negative comments reluctantly

People are generally more *shy about sharing* what they have labeled *negative comments* or unusual occurrences. These include falling asleep, not hearing, not getting into the meditation, or having a sexual fantasy. I strongly encourage at least some verbalization of "negatives"; people need to know that these experiences are all right. If no one names any of these phenomena, relate some yourself. Ask whether anyone had difficulty "seeing" anything or whether an image puzzled anyone. I try not to invade the privacy that a person chooses to maintain. I simply make clear my willingness to listen.

Ending in an awkward manner

Endings are awkward. Saying, "Open your eyes" seems abrupt, if people need to linger a little longer. I close with "Amen" more often now because that reminds a group that we are indeed praying. A nice bell would be appropriate for those who practice often enough for that to be a familiar, not surprising sound.

Bringing in assistance

People do *forget to bring in assistance.* Yet even without what they label assistance, they are tremendously creative in working through dilemmas that they encounter in the visualization. The leader needs to mention the possibility of calling on assistance *prior* to the practice. However, that guideline is seemingly irrelevant before one experiences the need for help.

Eliminating unnecessary and limiting details

I have occasionally included *details* that were *limiting and unnecessary.* I once referred to the gardener in the allegory of Jesus as the true vine, as "he." One person in the group had a female gardener. In that same meditation I said, "See the grapes," but several people had different fruit on their vines. Now I repeat the word *gardener* without using a pronoun and say *fruit* rather than *grapes.*

In one group, five out of eight people had difficulty planting a seed in sand. I had suggested that they were at the seashore in the parable of the self-growing seed. Each of the five found a creative solution to their logical dilemma, so their meditations were productive. However, now I suggest that people go wherever they want to plant the seed, so that they can find their appropriate soil and setting more easily.

Attending to these details is not a problem, if people realize that they do not need to obey the guiding words. However, the leader can minimize the potential inner confusion by keeping the guiding words as general as possible while staying within the intent of the meditation. Specific details are valuable for getting into a scene, but a fine line exists between unguided free association and overguided structuring.

Having a sense of realness

One fantastic and fun observation has been the *sense of reality* ascribed to the meditation scenes. People say, "When I was on the path . . ."; they seldom say, "When I imagined myself to be on the path. . . ."

DEBRIEFING AND GROUNDING: IDEAS AND TESTIMONIES

Untangling Images through Debriefing

Debriefing, expressing what occurred during the meditation either to others or privately on paper (in a journal or as a drawing) is an essential part of the guided meditation process. If we do not verbalize or write out what happened, we may not only forget the images, but more importantly, we may miss potential messages. One of the easiest ways to work toward finding significance is to consider three levels of meaning.[2]

I will illustrate this with a simple dream I had one night before I was to preach as a guest minister. In the dream when I walked up to the pulpit to preach, I could not see the people. I was too short to see over the pulpit. At the first level, an image is a direct message about the external world. A direct message from this dream would be that I should actually check the pulpit height when I arrive at a church to preach. Since I am short, it's good to check whether I can make eye contact with the people present.

The second level of meaning is an inner message about events in the external world. At this level, my dream may be advising me that I am not "seeing" the people or that I am "hiding" behind the pulpit in some fashion.

The third level of meaning is based entirely upon inner experience with no specific association to the external world. Using this dream, I might consider whether the part of me that identifies with the pulpit (perhaps the "preacher" or the "Ms. Authority" side of me) is overshadowing my "short," "female," or "humble" side.

If, as I practice the meditation "Toward Wholeness and Health," I see myself with irritated skin as I visualize myself at the healing pool, I can use the same three-level analysis. On the first level, the message may be telling me a fact about my world—I should take care of my skin. On the second level the message may be, "Something is getting under your skin!" That message is about my internal response to an external event. The third-level message relates entirely to my internal life: Perhaps it reflects an irritating barrier that I place at the boundary between myself and others.

The focus of the message can be at one level only; however, it can, and often does, relate to several levels of meaning simultaneously. I may be getting skin irritations because I erect (irritating) barriers between others and myself. I may let others "get under my skin." Because images are filled with puns, perhaps the image above is telling me that I am getting irritated over my need to be "skinny" or panicked by the need to decide whether or not to go "skinny dipping"!

Clearly, guidance from these imagery meditations is rarely straightforward. We have to *reflect* in order to glean relevant meanings.

When debriefing, remember to notice not just the content of the imagery scenes but the feeling tones or attitudes toward the images. "Two sailors stood on a raft while another raft floated toward them. Both jumped. The first said: I jumped from one raft to the other. The second said: I jumped over the sea."[3] It makes a lot of difference how we feel about the content in our images.

Visual images, feeling tones, puns, and aesthetic sensitivity are all parts of the full experience. Remember to pay attention to these aspects in the debriefing, just as in the meditation.

You may find help for debriefing imagery prayer in resources for understanding dreams. Currently I find two books by Jeremy Taylor most useful: *DreamWork: Techniques for Discovering the Creative Power in Dreams* and *Where People Fly and Water Runs Uphill*. John Sanford, Morton Kelsey, Ann Faraday, Patricia Garfield, Stephen LaBerge, and Eileen Stukane write helpful books in this area as well.[4] Edward Bynum has an excellent book, intended for use by families or family therapists: *Families and the Interpretation of Dreams*.

Growing through Group Study

The most facilitative attitude on the part of the leader is one of "intrigued delight" at what occurs: no judgment, just an acceptance of whatever persons tell about their meditations. At the same time, the leader should push meditators to ask themselves sincerely, "How does that image relate to my life?" To illustrate, a man commented that he saw "changing seasons" in his meditation. He thought these images were simply commenting on the fact that it was February—he was tired of winter. The facilitator suggested that he not be sure that his February analysis was the only meaning until he asked himself further questions. For example, "Were any seasons changing in his life?" In fact, the man was changing professions. Once he made this connection, he began talking about some of his feelings and faith questions related to the impending change. Debriefing after a meditation allows for theological discussion that is often more honest than abstract talk about beliefs because people are acutely aware of their own feelings and thoughts.

51

The interaction of group members can be enormously helpful during debriefing. One woman sought to rise out of the tomb of a rape experience. Others in the group took a glass jar and put stretched, "used" bandages into it. The attached note read, "Resurrection is possible." The one who sought healing was touched. She kept the jar to remind her of the love given by her friends and of God's healing energies.

A small group of Korean and Korean-American seminary students asked that I participate in their Bible study/prayer group one day. I was in the midst of preparing the meditation, "Holy, Humble, Indefatigable, and Healed," so I asked if the students would consider guided imagery meditation upon that passage. They agreed.

Three of their responses illustrate beautifully a typical sampling of experiences:

1. One man entered the house, found Jesus, who embraced him and said, "I love you." The meditator left the imaginary house, feeling his "self-esteem increased." He felt "valued."

2. Another entered the house of her imagination but could not find Jesus. There were a lot of people, too many to find Jesus. The meditator left the house, disappointed, feeling she had failed at the imagery.

3. A third person had a sense of peace, though he said he did not have specific images. In his words, "I didn't have any egoistic benefit but heard the benediction from Jesus, 'Go in peace.'"

In each case, asking about any link between the imagined scenario (being valued, not finding Jesus, and receiving a benediction) and the student's current life was fruitful. Often persons will see a connection. Many other insights are made as they share with one another.

Other humorous and group-building benefits can result from discussion. For example, we in the group I just mentioned realized that three of us—though we met and currently are living in Dayton, Ohio—had California beaches in our minds during the meditation (Long Beach, San Diego, and Malibu). This information fleshed out our personal histories.

Making Images Concrete through Grounding

The biblical passage and our personal imagery during the meditation are "extended metaphors" that we can call to mind more easily if we make an association with one concrete image. Having a key image, like a gift in the meditations "Reunion" or "The Gift of Reconciliation" or something that

52

"blooms" in "Blooming" provides a single image that can evoke the feeling tone or remembrance of other parts of the meditation.

Grounding refers to making concrete some of the images. Instead of having a "tremendous feeling" or a sense of "something ominous," we have a definite image to explore. Sermon titles function to summarize sermons. Long after we forget the details, we can recall the title, along with a feeling tone and perhaps some ideas within the sermon.

I remember one Christmas sermon preached by my pastor at the time, Dr. Cornish Rogers, which he entitled, "A Sky Full of Junk." I recall the image he painted with his words: the sky during Advent being filled with a star, Santa Claus, reindeer, and angels. Somehow that title and the sermon deeply affected me; just remembering the title brings back some of its potency. You may have had similar experiences with phrases or titles. One image from a meditation can produce a similarly long-lasting and profound effect.

Drawing images, looking for scenes to photograph, writing about the events that occurred in the meditation are all simple techniques of grounding. But you can be even more creative! Weave something with a particular design of significance, write a song with a meaningful lyric from the meditation, or dance a movement you noticed. You can "become" parts of your scenes, trying out what it is like to be first one aspect of the scene, then another. Try being the front door: "I am big and heavy. I provide protection. I am open." Or, "I am wooden, with locks, hard to open. But I like what I am."[5]

Make simple crafts. For example, if an imagery meditation opens a retreat, the leader may ask participants to draw an image on their name tags. When they introduce themselves, they also tell something about the image. Try more complex crafts, such as sculpture, masks, puppets, or cookie decorating, using images from the prayers.

With a group, murals are marvelous. People can sit around a table or on the floor while drawing the mural. Then after hanging it (or letting it remain as a center floor-piece) for all to see, individuals describe their drawings. Once I asked persons to draw images on a mural, but we did not share those immediately. At the close of the retreat, several people inquired about certain images, so we told about our drawings at that time. The images can surround a group for several weeks, especially if the group meets in its own room.

All of these ways of grounding a meditation require some forethought. You need to acquire the materials, and in many cases to distribute them, *before* the discussion of the biblical passage and *before* the meditation itself. In that way, persons are ready at the appropriate time.

While discussion is group-building, be careful that people only share what they really want to and try to prevent anyone from monopolizing the group's time. Individuals do not need to tell others about *all* of their prayer images. Privacy has its value too.

If you use these meditations in a worship setting, you may ground the experience in the following ways: (1) Take time to let two or three people speak in front of the whole group during the worship service. (2) Suggest that each person turn to a neighbor to discuss what occurred. (3) Encourage people to draw their images or to write. (Have paper ready, or use paper that is in the pews.) (4) Make a verbal commitment that you are available to work with anyone who feels the need to talk—after the service or soon. (5) Ask each person to commit herself or himself to sharing the experience with someone that day.

The Meditations

STEPS WHEN MEDITATING ALONE

1. Choose your place to meditate. Be sure you have freedom to concentrate.
2. Decide how much time you have to meditate. You might set a timer nearby but not so close to be a distraction. After you decide, let go of your concern for the time.
3. Choose the meditation you will use. Either move progressively through the book or browse through the indexes to find a meditation that suits your present needs. Instead, you may repeat one you have already experienced that feels unfinished or that was especially insightful.
4. Sit with an upright posture; straight, yet relaxed.
5. Remind yourself of the Eight Guidelines.
6. Take a few slow, deep breaths to relax.
7. Read the first three sections of the meditation: READING, BIBLICAL NOTE, and FOR YOUR MEDITATION.
8. Decide if you expect to work on any special areas during the meditation.
9. Take a few more slow, deep breaths to relax.
10. Do the meditation, using one of the following methods, or one you create. (The ellipses indicate times for pause.)
    - Alternate reading and closing your eyes in order to visualize.
    - Read the whole meditation several times, then visualize it as you remember it, without worrying whether you include every detail.
    - Tape-record the meditation in advance (reading aloud slowly), turning on the tape recorder now.
11. Sit in silence after the meditation.

12. Debrief and ground your experience.
    - Write in a journal.
    - Draw some part of the meditation.
    - Ask yourself how it relates to your current life situation.
    - Look at the three levels of meanings.
    - Share your reflections with a friend.

Decide whether you want to continue to work on something that emerged and how you will do that.

STEPS WHEN LEADING A GROUP

1. Reflect upon the setting in which this will be done (the number of people, time of day, seating arrangement, acoustical situation, etc.)
2. Decide how much time you have to practice the whole meditation (the introduction, the meditation, and the debriefing).
3. Choose the meditation to meet the needs of the people within that setting. The indexes offer guidelines for this.
4. Make any changes in the meditation that seem appropriate.
5. Call the group's attention to as many of the Eight Guidelines as is appropriate for the setting.
6. Pass out paper or anything you may use for the debriefing.
7. Call the group's attention to posture. Suggest an upright posture; straight, yet relaxed.
8. Discuss the three sections: READING, BIBLICAL NOTE, and FOR YOUR MEDITATION, as well as any further ideas you have on the passage or meditation.
9. Lead the group in a few slow, deep breaths for relaxation.
10. Lead the meditation slowly, in one of the following fashions (the ellipses indicate times for pause):
    - Read from this book.
    - Lead it from notes you have taken from the written meditation.
    - Lead it from your memory of doing it several times yourself, without worry about being exact.
    - Play a prerecorded tape of the written meditation.
11. Be silent after the meditation.
12. Debrief and ground the experience.
    - Share verbally.

- Draw, make a mural, or creatively express the experience in some other way.
- Write in individual journals.
- Ask how the meditation relates to immediate life situations.
- Recall the three levels of meanings.
- Enable individuals to decide upon further action.
- Check for any unfinished business—things that people have not yet mentioned but would like to.

FINDING A BURIED TREASURE

READING: "The kingdom of heaven is like treasure hidden in a field, which someone found and hid; then in his joy he goes and sells all that he has and buys that field" (Matthew 13:44).

BIBLICAL NOTE: The main vision of Jesus and his movement was that of the *basileia*, the kingdom or empire of God. All other groups in Palestine at that time shared the range of expectations evoked by the symbol—kingdom of God.

The rabbis in Jesus' time frequently told treasure stories, which are common in virtually every culture. The stories usually tell of a person who buys a field, then unexpectedly finds a treasure while working hard plowing. These stories were used in part to convey the orthodox theology of the time: Work hard and you will get more than you expect—you might even find God or the "kingdom," hidden here someplace.

In Jesus' parable, the person finds the treasure first! Then he buys the field and perhaps doesn't work at all. Mark Trotter, a United Methodist minister in San Diego, comments that this story "is an affront to religious piety and to morality." We are supposed to work first, then get the reward.[1]

Jesus' message is that the wholeness of God's people is already experientially available; God loves us now—regardless of our works.

FOR YOUR MEDITATION: Let yourself be open to *any* treasure that might appear. It may or may not immediately appear to be a symbol of the reign of God. (Meditation 39 picks up the theme of selling all else in order to have a treasure.)

MEDITATION: Take three slow, deep breaths and let yourself relax....Get a sense of yourself walking along a beach. . . . Feel the sand beneath your feet, its temperature and texture. . . . Feel the warmth of the sun, radiating upon your body. . . . Pay attention to what is around you on the beach. . . . As you walk, notice something that looks like a disturbance in the sand; push away the sand to find a buried treasure. . . . Do whatever you need to do to uncover that treasure. . . . Now as you open it, become aware of what is hidden within it. . . . Spend whatever time you need observing, becoming aware of, talking with or being with that treasure. . . . Let yourself participate in any way you want with that treasure. . . . Be aware of other things in your life and how they relate to this treasure. . . . You may encounter the Christ and talk about the treasure. . . . If you need to bring in other people or things, do that. . . . Follow through with this treasure in any way that feels right for you now. . . . Find some way to bring back with you a symbol of this treasure. . . . Walk back up the beach again, aware of the sand, the water, and the warm sun. . . . When you feel ready, open your eyes.

COMMENTS ON DEBRIEFING AND USE: For you, the treasure may be a talent that has lain dormant, a quality you wish to develop, a gift you can give to the world, an awareness of the "kingdom of God," or any number of other possibilities. If you practice this meditation several days in a row, you may find that you discover several different treasures. Or you may become more thoroughly acquainted with the same treasure.

You may want to limit "the treasure" to a symbol or awareness of the kingdom of God. I have not done this here because the kingdom of God may be an abstract notion to some, so it is difficult to visualize. The notion of "treasure" usually evokes a very concrete and positive finding.

If you did not find a treasure or if you found nothing within it, then simply accept that this is what occurred for you just now. First allow yourself to understand your feelings in not finding a treasure. Later you might choose to do the meditation again.

This meditation offers many exciting debriefing activities. You could make a box (or use a shoe box) and put your hidden treasure within the box in the form of a picture, a symbol, or in written words. You could sculpt your treasure. You could prepare a sandbox before the meditation. Afterward each participant submerges a symbol or words about his or her treasure. The participants then take turns "finding" one another's treasures. When found, the person whose symbol it is may share the meaning of it with the group. (I did this with fourth, fifth, and sixth graders in a Sunday school class; there was excitement in "finding" the symbols, even though the children had hidden them only shortly before.)

2

ALONG LIFE'S PATH

READING: So she said, "See, your sister-in-law has gone back to her people and to her gods; return after your sister-in-law." But Ruth said,

"Do not press me to leave you
or to turn back from following you!
Where you go, I will go;
Where you lodge, I will lodge;
your people shall be my people,
and your God my God.
Where you die, I will die—
there will I be buried.
May the Lord do thus and so to me,
and more as well,
if even death parts me from you!"

When Naomi saw that she was determined to go with her, she said no more to her (Ruth 1:15-18).

BIBLICAL NOTE: The name Ruth means "friend" or "companion" in Hebrew. Ruth exemplifies one who makes a covenant with God and the people of God.

To understand this particular passage, consider how Naomi and Ruth arrive at the moment of this interaction. Elimelech and Naomi were married and had two sons. Due to a famine in the land of Judah, Naomi, Elimelech, and their sons migrated to what looked like better lands—across the Dead Sea to the plains of Moab. Elimelech died; the two sons married Moabite wives (Orpah and Ruth). Then after ten years of marriage during which no children were born, both sons also died.

Naomi decides to return to her own country, leaving her two daughters-in-law in Moab. The women go with Naomi as she leaves; Ruth and Orpah do not want to say good-bye. Naomi urges them to return to their homes. Orpah agrees, but Ruth insists that she will follow Naomi, stating these famous words that are in our meditation: "Your people shall be my people, and your God my God."

After the passage upon which we are focusing, Ruth and Naomi go on to Judah, where Ruth gleans in the field of Boaz. (The farmers left the outside fringes of their land to be gleaned by the poor, the widows, and the orphans.) Boaz and Ruth fall in love, have a son, and their lineage descends to King David and finally to Jesus.

The Book of Ruth is one of five books of the Hebrew Scriptures that are read on different feast days in the Jewish tradition. (The other four books are The Song of Solomon, Ecclesiastes, Lamentations, and Esther.) Ruth is read for the Feast of Shavuot, the "Feast of Weeks," so named because it celebrates the end of the weeks of the grain harvest. The feast is also the day following the seven weeks after Passover. (In the Jewish tradition this festival is also called *Pentecost*, a word that in Greek means "fiftieth day"—the fiftieth day after Passover. In the Christian tradition, the numbering begins with Easter, and the fiftieth day is called Pentecost also.)

The story in Ruth is appropriate for the celebration of First Fruits, which celebrates God's ownership of the land and the annual gift of food, since a crucial part of the narrative takes place as Ruth gleans the fields during the barley harvest.

FOR YOUR MEDITATION: You could use this meditation in contexts that celebrate Jewish-Christian relations. The celebration of the Moabite (non-Jewish) Ruth on the Jewish equivalent of the Christian Pentecost shows how Judaism was willing to expand its boundaries to include outsiders.

Many find it valuable to think of their faith journey as a guided path. We find encouragement in knowing that God is not only offering guidance but consistently enticing us to follow it. We made choices yesterday that we cannot undo; some consequences cannot be changed. However, we have an open future. We are free to make new choices that are relevant to today's situation. We can walk in faith, knowing that God is with us.

You could use this meditation to enable members of a group to get to know one another or near the close of a group's existence; it could serve as a farewell blessing and anticipation of a hopeful future for each participant.

MEDITATION: Sit quietly and take at least three slow, deep breaths. . . . Get a sense of yourself being on your life path. . . . Notice the kind of path it is and how you are moving along it. . . . Look back and notice the kind of path on which you have traveled. Let yourself become aware of the decisions and choices you have made. . . . Now become aware of where you are today on your path. Look around and do whatever you need to do to get in touch with where you are today. . . . Become aware of the path ahead of you. . . . You do not know with any certainty where it leads or the choices that it will offer. Now remember Ruth and her decision. Let her come into your imagination—communicate with her about her choices and yours. . . . Get a sense of yourself being guided or nudged by God to make right choices. . . . You may want to walk ahead on the path, sensing yourself moving forward, experiencing this pull toward right decisions. . . . Ruth might come along with you, or you may invite another. If any particular decision emerges for you, pay attention to it and to your response. . . . Take whatever time you need to continue with as much looking forward as you want. . . . Now get a sense of the many people throughout the world who are following their unique paths. . . . You may especially pay attention to those in your family or those close to you. . . . Sense now the potential for right choices being made available to all. Say farewell to anyone you've invited into your imagery, knowing you can recall them to mind. Amen.

COMMENTS ON DEBRIEFING AND USE: If you draw the path and find that some particular part of it is unclear, go back into the meditation and work out that part of the path. You might act out your meditation, saying aloud, "I am now making this decision" as you had made it in the past. Then move forward to the present and as far toward the future as you care to imagine.

3

EXPANDING A QUALITY

READING: And again he said, "To what should I compare the kingdom of God? It is like yeast that a woman took and mixed in with three measures of flour until all of it was leavened." (Luke 13:20-21; see also Matthew 13:33).

BIBLICAL NOTE: Matthew 13 gives seven parables, one right after another: the sower of seeds, the weeds of the field, the mustard seed, the woman baking with yeast, the hidden treasure, the merchant searching for fine pearls, and the net and fish. The mustard seed and yeast parables sometimes are called "small to large" parables because they show how a tiny beginning can grow to amazing size.

Three measures of flour is also the amount that Sarah used to bake bread for the heavenly messengers in Genesis 18:6. This was the largest amount of dough a person could knead, about a bushel. One hundred people could eat the bread this woman would make!

Of the seven parables in Matthew, this is the only one in which a woman is the main character. Although the parables reinforced the division of labor that was probably practiced in that community at the time (women work inside, men outside), this parable shows how work associated with women was seen to be valuable.[2]

The realm of God has a small beginning, which is evident to Jesus' followers. Jesus may be indicating that this realm will become great, through the effort of those like this woman. Remember that the Jesus movement was known for its gathering around the table, sharing food and drink. Remember too that we celebrate in the Eucharist, "the bread of life."

FOR YOUR MEDITATION: Think of some quality in your life that you sense needs development. The quality might be patience, compassion, joy, serenity, humor, creativity, or something else that seems to reflect the realm of God. In order to decide which quality will be the basis of this meditation, you might become quiet, center in, then allow a quality to emerge. Or if you keep a journal, you may look through it for a quality you have mentioned. Think about the wisdom of expanding this quality in your life. Before you meditate, consider the ethical implications of this quality, the rightness of the timing, and your sense of commitment to developing it.

MEDITATION: Take three deep breaths as you sit upright in a comfortable position and allow yourself to relax. . . . Imagine yourself in a comfortable place where you can bake bread. This may be your home or any other comfortable setting for you. Notice colors, fragrances, and sounds. . . . Now visualize yeast, flour, water, eggs, salt, and any other ingredients you need as you anticipate baking bread. Put the yeast into the water and let it rise while you prepare the flour mixture. When the yeast has risen, stir it into the dry ingredients. Add eggs or other special ingredients. Knead. Let the dough rise. . . . When it is double its original size, punch it down and shape it as you desire, then bake the bread. . . . As you take the bread out of the oven, observe its quality. . . .

Now again look at your comfortable place. . . . Remind yourself of the quality you have chosen to develop. . . . Remember a time when you experienced this quality in some measure in your life. . . . Let yourself experience that quality as you did then. . . . Let this be your yeast. Now imagine moving through your daily routine, expressing this quality in a large measure. As yeast permeates the bread, let this quality permeate your day. . . . [long pause] Notice the effect on other people as you radiate this quality. . . . Sit, simply aware of this quality's permeating your being, radiating through you and all that you do. . . . When you feel ready, open your eyes.

COMMENTS ON DEBRIEFING AND USE: Visualizing the bread making first generally helps one to go on to the more abstract visualization of living out a quality. If you repeat this meditation, you may find that you want to omit the yeast section and simply visualize the quality, thinking through a day in which you are living out that quality more fully.

This meditation is a good one to use in worship when you celebrate Communion. A group could prepare the bread for Communion. (If members practiced this meditation while baking, a few could share their images with the congregation.) Slides could illustrate bread's rising. If the bread is freshly baked at the church, its aroma would enhance the atmosphere.

Write the quality in the middle of a clean sheet of paper. Then, while focusing upon that, write other words that you associate with that quality as spokes to a wheel with the original quality as the hub. Do this again, starting afresh but using the same quality daily for a week to a month. Review the papers to observe how the quality has transformed or affected you over time.

Most people who meditate in order to develop a certain quality agree that it takes at least two months to observe that quality's becoming a central part of their life. Thus, doing this meditation over a period of time increases its benefits.

4

REFLECTIONS UPON YOUR SEEDS

READING: Again he began to teach beside the sea. Such a very large crowd gathered around him that he got into a boat on the sea and sat there, while the whole crowd was beside the sea on the land. He began to teach them many things in parables, and in his teaching he said to them: "Listen! A sower went out to sow. And as he sowed, some seed fell on the path, and the birds came and ate it up. Other seed fell on rocky ground, where it did not have much soil, and it sprang up quickly, since it had no depth of soil. And when the sun rose, it was scorched; and since it had no root, it withered away. Other seed fell among thorns, and the thorns grew up and choked it, and it yielded no grain. Other seed fell into good soil and brought forth grain, growing up and increasing and yielding thirty and sixty and a hundredfold." And he said, "Let anyone with ears to hear listen!" (Mark 4:1-9; see also Matthew 13:1-9, 18-23; Luke 8:4-8; and the Gospel of Thomas 82:3-13.)

BIBLICAL NOTE: For the writer of Mark's Gospel, this parable points to the fact that suffering and violence are part of the divinely created order.[3] It is assumed that some things will go wrong. There is no explanation about evil, lack of productivity, or infertility. These are mysteries, part of the way life is. All the sower can do is to sow the seeds, and the sower will "succeed" only so often. Not all the seeds will take root. God will take care of the whole situation.

Matthew offers two versions of this parable, both told in a boat on "the sea," probably Galilee. Jesus' words about the purpose of parables in general separate the versions. The second version, found in Matthew 13:18-23, becomes an allegory that focuses upon the soil, comparing a type of soil with a type of person.

FOR YOUR MEDITATION: This meditation affirms the past, with its mixed experiences; and the future, with its potential.

Hand four seeds to each person before starting this meditation. This tangible element enhances the ability to focus.

MEDITATION: Take a few deep breaths. Get a sense of yourself on a small hill by a lake. . . . Feel the warmth of the sun. . . . Now, as you look toward the beach, you see people gathered. . . . Notice the Christ standing on a boat, talking to the people. . . . You go down the hill to the shore. . . . As you watch and listen, you hear the Christ talk about seeds that represent how one responds to the gospel. Some seeds fall along footpaths, some on the rocky ground, some among the thistles, and some in good soil. . . .

The Christ gives everyone four seeds. . . . Receive your seeds and move away from the crowd to any place that feels right to sow your seeds. . . . Now throw these four seeds, allowing them to land where they will.

The first seed lands upon a footpath. The birds come and eat it up. Reflect upon something in your life that was plucked up before it had a full chance to grow. . . . Be aware of your feelings. . . .

The second seed lands upon rocky soil; it takes root but dies quickly because it has no depth. As you see this seed grow, then die, allow it to represent something in your life that withered because it was not securely rooted. . . . Notice your experience. . . .

The third seed lands and grows but is choked out by thistles. Become aware of something in your life that other interests, activities, or values have choked out.

Your fourth seed lands, takes root in good soil, grows, and bears fruit. Watch this take place. . . . Now observe what in your life has borne great fruit. Get a sense of that ripe fruit. . . . Watch it; allow it to unfold even more. Become aware that seeds are being sown all around the world by diverse people. . . . Imagine the bearing of much good fruit. Notice your present surroundings; when you are ready, open your eyes.

COMMENTS ON DEBRIEFING AND USE: Draw the four seeds. If you are in a group, you could prepare a mural with images from the many seeds, then discuss the drawings with their accompanying meanings.

Sometimes it helps to ask people to jot down notes or draw sketches after each of the four sections of this prayer, for it is difficult to retain the memory of what all four seeds represent at the completion of the meditation.

5

ENCOUNTERING GOD—
RECEIVING A MISSION

READING: Moses was keeping the flock of his father-in-law Jethro, the priest of Midian; he led his flock beyond the wilderness, and came to Horeb, the mountain of God. There the angel of the Lord appeared to him in a flame of fire out of a bush; he looked, and the bush was blazing, yet it was not consumed. Then Moses said, "I must turn aside and look at this great sight, and see why the bush is not burned up." When the Lord saw that he had turned aside to see, God called to him out of the bush, "Moses, Moses!" And he said, "Here I am." Then he said, "Come no closer! Remove the sandals from your feet, for the place on which you are standing is holy ground. . . ."

Then the Lord said, "I have observed the misery of my people who are in Egypt; I have heard their cry on account of their taskmasters. Indeed, I know their sufferings, and I have come down to deliver them from the Egyptians, and to bring them up out of that land to a good and broad land, a land flowing with milk and honey. . . . So come, I will send you to Pharaoh to bring my people, the Israelites, out of Egypt." But Moses said to God, "Who am I that I should go to Pharaoh and bring the Israelites out of Egypt?" He said, "I will be with you; and this shall be the sign for you that it is I who sent you: when you have brought the people out of Egypt, you shall worship God on this mountain" (Exodus 3:1-5, 7-8, 10-12).

BIBLICAL NOTE: At the time of this passage, Moses has just gotten adjusted to the life of a shepherd. He is in the midst of his daily work when God appears to him unexpectedly, disrupting his routine. Apparently Moses was not looking for a "mountaintop" experience or pondering God's guidance for his life.

This is a "call narrative," a story about how a person is called by God.

Biblical calls generally include a commission, an objection ("Who am I?"), a reassurance, and a sign. This story has all four dimensions. Moses gains a new perspective on life that enables him to follow the call. These biblical narratives always arise out of a specific situation and present a concrete task to be done. Here Moses was to lead the Israelites out of Egypt.

Objections to the call are natural and orthodox. They remind us that we humans are inadequate to fulfill any divine call and that we naturally want to avoid the risk involved. The objection brings divine reassurance. Notice that the assurance is not that Moses will succeed, nor is it a commendation of Moses' abilities. God simply promises to be with Moses, to share the risk, even if Moses fails.

FOR YOUR MEDITATION: You might act out this meditation as well as imagine it in your mind. Some teenagers who practiced this meditation were enthusiastic about the encounter with God. However, they had a much more difficult time expressing their mission to the world. I decided that it would be helpful to discuss world concerns and what could be done about them *before* such a meditation.

MEDITATION: Become quiet and take a few slow, deep breaths. Become aware of yourself in your daily routine. . . . You notice something that catches your attention. . . . You turn aside; as you turn, you hear God speak to you. . . . God speaks your name. . . . You respond. . . . God tells you to take off your shoes, for this is holy ground; you do that. . . . God tells you that God has seen some concern in your life or the life of others. God mentions this; you listen. . . . God informs you that you can do something about it, and you listen. . . . You question what you can do. . . . Allow yourself to ask any questions that you want. . . . Share any doubts that you might feel or any other concerns or hopes. . . . Allow God to reassure you that God is with you always. . . . Allow yourself to sense this. . . . Communicate anything else that seems necessary. When you are ready, finish your dialogue with God and continue with your daily routine. Think back on what has occurred. . . . Open your eyes.

COMMENTS ON DEBRIEFING AND USE: Grounding could include discussion about drawings, murals, or paintings of the events. Or you could role-play, enact, what happened. Be sure to give attention to the guidance received for action.

6

Feeling Like Grasshoppers
or Giants

READING: But Caleb quieted the people before Moses, and said, "Let us go up at once and occupy it, for we are well able to overcome it." Then the men who had gone up with him said, "We are not able to go up against this people, for they are stronger than we." So they brought to the Israelites an unfavorable report of the land that they had spied out, saying, "The land that we have gone through as spies is a land that devours its inhabitants; and all the people that we saw in it are of great size; . . . and to ourselves we seemed like grasshoppers, and so we seemed to them." . . .

And Joshua . . . and Caleb, . . . who were among those who had spied out the land, tore their clothes and said to all the congregation of the Israelites, "The land that we went through as spies is an exceedingly good land. If the Lord is pleased with us, he will bring us into this land and give it to us, a land that flows with milk and honey. Only, do not rebel against the Lord; and do not fear the people of the land, for they are no more than bread for us; their protection is removed from them, and the Lord is with us; do not fear them." But the whole congregation threatened to stone them (Numbers 13:30-33; 14:6-10).

BIBLICAL NOTE: Numbers 13 and 14 tell how Moses and the Israelites investigate the "promised" land. The spies they send into the land come back with two reports. The majority says the land is fertile, but that the people there are giants, stronger than they; the Israelites seemed like grasshoppers in comparison. Joshua and Caleb make the minority report—there is a great army in the land, but it is an exceedingly good land and, with God's help, the Israelites could take it.

FOR YOUR MEDITATION: This story is about battle, invasion for land. While today we would differ with the rights to invade another territory to take the land, we can use this story as a metaphor for things in our lives that seem "far off," giant, just beyond our horizons.

The new challenge may be attending college, applying for a particular position, remodeling a home, seeking ordination, or starting a process toward healing[4] (medical treatments, counseling, family therapy, an addiction recovery program, or an exercise plan). This challenge could be a collective one, such as working for sustainable lifestyles on earth, feeding the hungry, housing the homeless, or providing health care for all.

MEDITATION: If possible, slowly stretch your arms, legs, torso; then let your body relax. Take several deep, slow breaths as you come to a comfortable, attentive position. Visualize a large open space. . . . Imagine expanses not yet visible beyond the horizon. Allow to come to mind a decision or challenge that you are considering. . . . Imagine that decision or challenge to be just beyond the horizon. . . . Either go yourself, in your imagination, or send several "spies" to check out that area beyond the horizon. . . . Once there, see how fertile it is. . . . Notice obstacles to your claiming what is there in that land. . . .

Return or bring back your spies in your imagination. . . . Let yourself experience the debate about what to do. . . . The debate may be with or without words. Notice who argues for what decision. . . . You may come to some inner conviction, or you may not. Scan the vast open space again, seeking discernment or confirmation. Notice who is with you. Recall that God is with you. Take several deep, slow breaths and open your eyes, aware of your environment and God's presence in your room.

COMMENTS ON DEBRIEFING AND USE: Of course this story of the Israelites was written after the events—in part to explain them. The Israelites, we are told, made a decision between two choices: go into the land and try to occupy it or do not invade the land. Actually, whether or not they realized it at the time, the Israelites had more options!

For your decision, be wary of the idea that you either have to say yes or no. Part of your debriefing may include making a list of more creative options. Remember that the images may be clues to divine guidance. Using our God-given reasoning capacities and receiving honest feedback from others enable more clues to develop which, when added to the images, can help the discernment process.

7

TOWARD WHOLENESS AND HEALTH

READING: After this there was a festival of the Jews, and Jesus went up to Jerusalem. Now in Jerusalem by the Sheep Gate there is a pool, called in Hebrew Beth-zatha, which has five porticoes. In these lay many invalids—blind, lame, and paralyzed. One man was there who had been ill for thirty-eight years. When Jesus saw him lying there and knew that he had been there a long time, he said to him, "Do you want to be made well?" The sick man answered him, "Sir, I have no one to put me into the pool when the water is stirred up; and while I am making my way, someone else steps down ahead of me." Jesus said to him, "Stand up, take your mat and walk." At once the man was made well, and he took up his mat and began to walk (John 5:1-9).

BIBLICAL NOTE: The gospel in its earliest form insisted that Jesus claimed that the *basileia* (reign of God) is for three groups of people: the destitute poor; the sick and crippled; and tax collectors, sinners, and prostitutes. Here a man lay beside the pool, waiting to be the first to jump in when the water was "stirred up." In ancient times, people believed that a local divinity's presence caused the disturbance in the water. Jewish people changed that to suggest that an angel was present and that the first person to bathe in the pool would be cured. Since this man was lame, he could never get there first—someone always entered before him.

FOR YOUR MEDITATION: Think of some particular part of your body in which you desire to have greater health. Or if you would like to think of this emotionally, intellectually, or spiritually, consider some aspect of your life in which you desire wholeness.

MEDITATION: Sit quietly and take a few slow, deep breaths. . . . Allow the tension in your body to be released. . . . Imagine yourself by a pool of water. . . . Notice who is with you beside this pool. . . . Notice the edge of

72

the pool. . . . Look at the water and notice the color, the temperature, the texture. . . . Notice the details of this pool. . . . Now become aware of your own body and of a particular area for which you desire health. . . . Observe the Christ walking toward you, sitting down beside you, and asking you what you are doing. You respond, telling the Christ why you are there. . . . The Christ asks you if you want to be made whole. . . . Feel free to interact. Communicate in any way that feels right for you. . . . Decide with the Christ what you are going to do. . . . You may get up, affirm your wholeness, and walk on home. You may move into the water and swim around, splashing, feeling the cleansing and healing of your body. Or you may come to understand some guidance about the present and future state of your health. . . . Let yourself finish this scene as it feels right for you. Stay in touch with the quality of health and wholeness that surrounds the water in this pool and the faith conviction that you and the Christ share. . . . Know that you can return to this setting in your imagination whenever you want. . . . When you are ready, open your eyes.

COMMENTS ON DEBRIEFING AND USE: Practice of this meditation may aid the process of healing within your body, emotions, mind, and spirit. I would suggest using this meditation daily—two or three times if you are working on a major challenge. If you practice this meditation in a group, a discussion of healing is important. We can think of prayer and meditation as facilitating the natural healing and immunizing process of our body rather than as giant pills to bring instant cures. Although I am aware that so-called miraculous cures do occur, I would rather foster a hope in long-term well-being than a hope in instant healing. A woman friend of mine who is sixty walks with the aid of one crutch. She has the use of only one arm, due to having polio as a teenager. With her one arm, she swings her hips and walks well. She told me that people have asked her whether she would like them to pray so that she could walk. She responds, "It's a miracle—I do!" Healing takes many forms.

8

THE GIFT OF RECONCILIATION

READING: So when you are offering your gift at the altar, if you remember that your brother or sister has something against you, leave your gift there before the altar and go; first be reconciled to your brother or sister, and then come and offer your gift (Matthew 5:23-24).

BIBLICAL NOTE: This teaching, mentioned only in Matthew, is set in the midst of several comments by Jesus about how to fulfill the Law. Jesus has greater concern for what is inside the person, their motives and attitudes, than he does for their observable outward behavior.

FOR YOUR MEDITATION: Practicing this meditation regularly helps you discharge accumulated feelings that limit your joy in life. You might find this meditation especially helpful just before a particularly stressful family gathering or worrisome event at work.

A congregation could practice this meditation just prior to receiving tithes and offerings or as the prayer of confession or statement of forgiveness. It need not be thought of only individually—a group (people of one race in a community or one segment of an institution) may desire reconciliation with another group.

MEDITATION: Take a few deep breaths to relax and center in. . . . Now get a sense of yourself being at a beautiful temple or sacred place. . . . Notice the structure, colors, fragrances, and people who are there. . . . Allow yourself to absorb the beauty, the dignity, the sense of majesty. . . . Now become aware that you have a gift in your hand. . . . Walk up toward the altar and place the gift upon the altar. While you are there, standing or kneeling, consider whether there is anyone who has something against you. . . . Become aware of that unfinished business, whatever it may be. . . . Now walk back down the aisle of the temple or sacred place to go to that person with whom you do not have peace. . . .

Encounter that person and communicate in whatever way is most effective. . . . If needed, you can always ask for assistance in order to communicate. . . . Let yourself interact. . . .

When you feel ready, return to the sacred place or temple and go up to the altar. . . . Again reflect to see if there is anyone with whom you have unfinished business. . . . If so, go out again, find that person, and communicate with him or her. . . . Again return to the temple and go up to the altar. Once more become aware of the majesty within this place and the sense of cleansing reconciliation. Sense God's all-pervading love moving through you. Now offer the gift you had placed at the altar and experience its being accepted. When you feel ready, move out of the temple and into your daily life. . . . Open your eyes.

COMMENTS ON DEBRIEFING AND USE: You may have to practice this meditation several times before you come to the point where you want to face or talk with a particular person. You may also find that when you practice this meditation the second, third, or fifteenth time, you continue to find more people with whom to reconcile.

Notice that Matthew uses the word *reconciled* rather than *forgiveness*. This meditation is not intended to force forgiveness. At times people feel guilty because they just can't forgive, as their well-meaning friends tell them (or as they tell themselves) they are supposed to do. Forgiveness is not an act of the will—we can't make it happen. Usually we ponder, refeel a situation, experience anger, try to gain a larger perspective, imagine ourselves into the life of the other person, then eventually realize that we have in large measure forgiven. Forgiveness does not mean forgetting entirely or condoning. It means that we no longer wrap our identity around that crisis; the hurtful event has moved to the periphery of our experience, out of the center. Forgiveness and reconciliation are processes like scars, improving regularly but always "having been there."[5]

Draw the temple, the people with whom you interacted, or the gift.

9

MIGHTY OR MITE OFFERINGS

READING: He sat down opposite the treasury, and watched the crowd putting money into the treasury. Many rich people put in large sums. A poor widow came and put in two small copper coins, which are worth a penny. Then he called his disciples and said to them, "Truly I tell you, this poor widow has put in more than all those who are contributing to the treasury. For all of them have contributed out of their abundance, but she out of her poverty has put in everything she had, all she had to live on" (Mark 12:41-44; see also Luke 21:1-4).

BIBLICAL NOTE: The two coins the widow gave were *leptons*, the least valuable coins in use at the time. Even then all widows were not poor. Some wealthy widows were influential members of early Christian communities. However, widows were defenseless because, no longer having husbands, they were not protected financially or legally. It is interesting that just prior to this event at the Temple, Jesus had condemned the scribes for consuming the homes of widows (see Mark 12:40). (There was a practice of appointing a man to oversee the affairs of a widow, but sometimes these supposedly pious men used the estate for their own benefit.)

The widow gave all that she had without drawing attention to herself. By so doing, she made herself even more vulnerable with regard to wealth, security, or status.

An overarching dimension of this vignette is Jesus' teaching about the coming of the end of the world, which occurs just after this passage in Mark. Her behavior makes sense as an act of faith in the coming reign of God.

FOR YOUR MEDITATION: Clearly this meditation would be valuable when a congregation's focus is on stewardship—on "Stewardship Sunday" or when a congregation faces a financial decision. However this is a meaningful meditation for use any time before the giving of tithes and offerings. With some creativity, congregations could use this meditation when receiving new members, when renewing baptismal vows, or when asking the members to consider avenues of service for the coming year.

In The United Methodist Church those who join promise to give of their prayers, presence, gifts, and service. (Many denominations have similar vows.) While this biblical passage appears to relate only to financial gifts, we could discuss the feeling of having a "mite" of service or, for some, a "mite" of presence.

Whether wealthy, comfortable, vulnerable, or very poor, an individual or family could use this mediation to gain perspective on attachment to wealth, security, or status. Using our imagination to confront our attachments can stretch our faith.

MEDITATION: Take a few deep breaths, slowly allowing clean air to enter and permeate your body. Let the air leave slowly, taking with it stress, worry, or tension.

Visualize a temple-like setting . . . perhaps a place of worship that is currently important for you or a sacred place from your past. [If you are in a congregational setting, you may name that particular local church here.] Notice people coming and going, sharing their gifts. Some give a great deal. One woman, a widow, gives a penny; you realize that is all she has. You notice that the Christ is beside you. You discuss the gift of this widow and her faith. Take a while to dialogue with the Christ.

Now imagine yourself to be one of the persons in this scene: a wealthy person, the widow, or even the Christ. Imagine what it is like to give what you have to offer. How does it feel? How do you respond to others? How do you feel about yourself? Imagine the future as you consider Jesus' words about the nearness of God's reign.

Return to the scene as yourself. Receive guidance regarding your own giving or about your attitude toward money, security, or status. . . . You may want to dialogue with another person. . . .

Continue until you feel the exchange is complete, knowing that you can reenter the scene to continue the dialogue whenever you choose.

Become aware of many people nearby and far away who wrestle, as you do, with their security and their gift giving. Consider your sense of trust in the future. Amen.

COMMENTS ON DEBRIEFING AND USE: In our society many people still equate affluence with divine favor. This prayer helps one to gain perspective, placing a person within his or her family and cultural context but also within the frame of reference of God's reign. A discussion of these issues may be fruitful after individuals have, in their imagination, empathized with a different person.

You may write your name in the middle of a sheet of paper, then write or draw what it is that you give (in prayer, presence, gifts, and service) to your church, your family, and the larger community.

10

BEFRIENDING THE TIMES IN OUR LIVES

READING:
> Send out your bread upon the waters,
>> for after many days you will get it back.
>
> Divide your means seven ways, or even eight,
>> for you do not know what disaster may happen on earth.
>
> When clouds are full,
>> they empty rain on the earth;
>
> whether a tree falls to the south or to the north,
>> in the place where the tree falls, there it will lie.
>
> Whoever observes the wind will not sow;
>> and whoever regards the clouds will not reap.

Just as you do not know how the breath comes to the bones in the mother's womb, so you do not know the work of God, who makes everything.

In the morning sow your seed, and at evening do not let your hands be idle; for you do not know which will prosper, this or that, or whether both alike will be good.

Light is sweet, and it is pleasant for the eyes to see the sun.

Even those who live many years should rejoice in them all; yet let them remember that the days of darkness will be many. All that comes is vanity (Ecclesiastes 11:1-8).

BIBLICAL NOTE: Qohelet, the one who assembled the people together to teach, authored what we now call the Book of Ecclesiastes. This one observed that all is a "puff of air," "breathlike," "fleeting." The original word *hebel* in Hebrew conveyed this sense of lack of permanence. However the Hebrew was translated to Greek, influenced by Latin, and then translated to English. The word we often see in our biblical translations is *vanity*, which implies more a lack of value than a lack of permanence.

"All is *hebel*" is ambiguous. It could mean, "all is worthless, meaningless, or futile." But in a relatively positive light, we may understand it to mean "all is fleeting" under the sun. God is permanent. All else is transitory.

A dominant theme through all of Ecclesiastes is that we should not worry about getting permanent results. We should simply enjoy life with all its ambiguity, during every season and at every age. Qohelet believes that God intends for us to "take pleasure" in what we do during our brief lives on earth. Qohelet does not believe that anything goes but advises his audience to relax and enjoy their fleeting lives. Rather than insisting that God's judgment is accomplished on earth in what we see "under the sun," the Assembler suggests that we might as well enjoy what work we have been given to do and leave whatever comes "after" to God. (See Kathleen A. Farmer's excellent commentary on Ecclesiastes, *Who Knows What Is Good?: A Commentary on the Books of Proverbs and Ecclesiastes.*)

FOR YOUR MEDITATION: Every scripture passage presents a theological view; our Bible is more like a library of theologies than one book with one point of view. Allow yourself to enter this meditation with your own theology. You may debate Qohelet, agree, or suggest an alternate view. This meditation is enjoyable for a group composed of several generations, for they learn from one another.

MEDITATION: Move your body in swaying motions, shaking parts like your shoulders, hands, and feet to let them relax. Take at least four deep breaths slowly, no rushing.

Imagine yourself in some comfortable outdoor setting. Now you hear a preacher named Qohelet saying, "Send out your bread upon the waters, for after many days you will get it back." Imagine that. Consider what in your life is "bread" that you send forth and which, likewise, returns to you. . . .

Now you hear, "Divide your means seven ways, or even eight, for you do not know what disaster may happen on earth." Consider that. Imagine ways you are prepared for crises or disasters. . . . See yourself being flexible, able to handle crises. If you are particularly afraid of disasters, reflect upon what gets in your way of accepting them as part of life.

Qohelet continues, "whether a tree falls to the south or to the north, in the place where the tree falls, there it will lie." Imagine a tree's falling. Consider the significance of what direction it falls. Now let an event that you are anticipating come to your imagination. Try seeing it happen this way, then that. Notice how you experience the different options. See if you can appreciate the various outcomes or what gets in the way of your accepting it as it happens. . . .

Notice your age, how old you are. What do you rejoice in at this age? Let some images come to mind. . . . Consider that being this old is like a "puff of air," relatively brief. Consider being a little older. Notice in what you will rejoice when you are a little older. . . . Let yourself rejoice.

Smile. Move your body gently, and open your eyes.

COMMENTS ON DEBRIEFING AND USE: Draw the "bread," which you send forth and which returns to you. Also draw how you are prepared for crises and what gets in your way of accepting them as a natural part of life. Name or draw the various possible outcomes of the upcoming event you considered, as well as your potential responses.

Draw yourself at your current age, doing or being what you enjoy at this time. Draw yourself at earlier and future ages, rejoicing in what that stage offers. If possible, share experiences across generations.

11

Calming the Storm Within

Reading:
> Then they cried to the Lord in their trouble,
>> and he brought them out from their distress;
> he made the storm be still,
>> and the waves of the sea were hushed.
> Then they were glad because they had quiet,
>> and he brought them to their desired haven.
> Let them thank the Lord for his steadfast love,
>> for his wonderful works to humankind.
> Let them extol him in the congregation of the people,
>> and praise him in the
>>> assembly of the elders (Psalm 107: 28-32).

Biblical Note: In Judaism and the early Christian church, people read the Psalms as scripture, recited them as prayers, and sang them as hymns. This psalm is a communal psalm of thanksgiving. The priest seems to be calling the congregation together to celebrate a festival. Probably pilgrims had traveled from various places to celebrate. Those who had crossed deserts had received food and discernment; those in prison were visited and comforted with the sense of God's presence; those who had been sick were healed; and those who came across the sea had survived storms.

For Your Meditation: The portion of Psalm 107 focused upon for this meditation relates to the calming of a storm. You could use the whole psalm or another portion (regarding the desert, prison, or sickness), if those are more relevant to your situation.

The storms you are most likely to think about are probably metaphorical ones—you have been through stormy times—individually or as a family, congregation, or community. However after a thunderstorm, earthquake, tornado, or other earthly crisis, this psalm would be relevant on the physical level too. Communities that have weathered such storms need opportunities to name their feelings, to grieve, to heal. This meditation could help.

This Bible translation uses the term *desired haven*; other translations convey the idea that the people were guided to a harbor. In the meditation, this haven or harbor can be any safe place to which you return.

MEDITATION: Take three or more slow deep breaths and get in touch with the presence of God. Now visualize yourself in a boat. . . . Notice the size and type of boat. . . . Observe who is with you. . . . Become aware of how you feel being there. . . . Now the water is becoming troubled, a storm begins to surround you. . . . Stay in touch with your feelings amidst this storm. . . .

Now sense a Calming Presence in your midst. . . . You might call out to that Presence to calm the storm, or you might realize that the Presence is calming the storm. . . . Experience the storm's calming and reflect on how you feel and what is occurring. . . . Now move into the safe harbor, staying alert to your feelings and thoughts as your boat nudges toward safety. . . . Before you disembark, look around on the boat for a symbol or image that represents this safety or calm for you. Take that symbol with you as you get off the boat. . . . Become aware of your thankfulness for the Loving Presence that enables that calm. . . . When you feel ready, open your eyes.

COMMENTS ON DEBRIEFING AND USE: If you had a clear image or symbol to bring back from the boat, draw it. Think about that image—how it represents calmness for you. Draw both the stormy picture and the calm picture. Hang the pictures in some obvious place to help you remember these experiences. Write down how this deep sense of calm affects a "storm" in your life right now. Notice any changes in attitude toward the storm in your life.

If you were unable to arrive at calmness, acknowledge that this is how you are right now. Feel free to practice this meditation again soon. Also feel free to write out the stormy feelings.

12

LET YOUR LIGHT SHINE

READING: "You are the light of the world. A city built on a hill cannot be hid. No one after lighting a lamp puts it under the bushel basket, but on the lampstand, and it gives light to all in the house. In the same way, let your light shine before others, so that they may see your good works and give glory to your Father in heaven" (Matthew 5:14-16; see also Mark 4:21-23 for a similar teaching and John 8:12 for reference to Jesus as light).

BIBLICAL NOTE: *The light of the world* is a phrase that rabbis used when naming God, Israel, or the Torah. Notice that Mark 4:21-23 talks about not hiding the lamp but does not speak directly to the hearer—it does not say, as Matthew does, "you." The Gospel of John refers to Jesus' saying, "I am the light of the world. Whoever follows me will never walk in darkness but will have the light of life."

FOR YOUR MEDITATION: Throughout history, light has served as a symbol to represent the divine or some aspect of the divine, such as radiance or wisdom. Before entering a home, a hospital room, or a class-room, I like to imagine the place filled with the warm radiance of light—God. It becomes a prayer of illumination, healing, or enlightenment.

MEDITATION: Become quiet and take a few deep, slow breaths. . . . Now picture yourself in a grassy area. . . . The sun is shining, penetrating your skin. . . . You walk through the grassy area, aware of the colors, fragrances, and sights around you. . . . You come to a dwelling of some kind, a structure. . . . Stand before the structure, observing the details from outside. . . . Notice what the door is like, of what the structure is made, what color and texture it is. . . . When you have observed the outside, walk up to the front door, open it, and slowly walk inside. . . . You notice a lamp; light it. . . . Sense the light's moving throughout the whole place. That light is illuminating the whole structure. . . . Stand, observing that lamp, becoming aware that you too are radiating your presence throughout this place. Identify with the quality of light. . . .

Now look for a place where you could put the lamp to make it shine more brightly throughout this structure. . . . Observe the intensity of the light permeating through the structure. . . . Get a sense of yourself radiating like this light. If there is a place anywhere at all where you could be brighter, like the lamp, go ahead and put yourself there, even if it is outside this dwelling. If you need any assistance to get there, you may ask for any help you need or want. . . . Keep in touch with the quality of light that you are radiating. . . . If you would be brighter by facing in a certain direction, then turn that way. . . . Do whatever you need to do to let your light shine. . . . Look at your surroundings and see how your light affects the surroundings.

Keep in touch with the quality of light that you are radiating. . . . Remember what has occurred. . . . When you feel ready, open your eyes.

COMMENTS ON DEBRIEFING AND USE: Sketch the lamp in the dwelling and yourself in your brightest environment.

This meditation would be compatible with worship that is held in candlelight. Or practice this meditation along with the meditation "Feeding the Hungry" (Meditation 33) at an event that deals with world concerns.

13

Being Known and Knowing Christ

READING: A Samaritan woman came to draw water, and Jesus said to her, "Give me a drink." (His disciples had gone to the city to buy food.) The Samaritan woman said to him, "How is it that you, a Jew, ask a drink of me, a woman of Samaria?" (Jews do not share things in common with Samaritans.) Jesus answered her, "If you knew the gift of God, and who it is that is saying to you, 'Give me a drink,' you would have asked him, and he would have given you living water." The woman said to him, "Sir, you have no bucket, and the well is deep. Where do you get that living water? Are you greater than our ancestor Jacob, who gave us the well, and with his sons and his flocks drank from it?" Jesus said to her, "Everyone who drinks of this water will be thirsty again, but those who drink of the water that I will give them will never be thirsty. The water that I will give will become in them a spring of water gushing up to eternal life." The woman said to him, "Sir, give me this water, so that I may never be thirsty or have to keep coming here to draw water."

Jesus said to her, "Go, call your husband, and come back." The woman answered him, "I have no husband." Jesus said to her, "You are right in saying, 'I have no husband'; for you have had five husbands, and the one you have now is not your husband. What you have said is true!" The woman said to him, "Sir, I see that you are a prophet. Our ancestors worshiped on this mountain, but you say that the place where people must worship is in Jerusalem." Jesus said to her, "Woman, believe me, the hour is coming when you will worship the Father neither on this mountain nor in Jerusalem. You worship what you do not know; we worship what we know, for salvation is from the Jews." . . . The woman said to him, "I know that Messiah is coming" (who is called Christ). "When he comes, he will proclaim all things to us." Jesus said to her, "I am he, the one who is speaking to you."

Just then his disciples came. They were astonished that he was speaking with a woman. . . . Then the woman left her water jar and went back to the city. She said to the people, "Come and see a man who told me everything I have ever done! He cannot be the Messiah, can he?" They left the city and were on their way to him (John 4:7-22, 25-30).

BIBLICAL NOTE: This is a beautiful interchange between a "foreign" woman and Jesus; one in which she is known by him, and he becomes known by her. They recognize the true humanity—and divinity—that is present. Many commentators and preachers have imposed upon this text the idea that the woman has a naughty or immoral past or present. Yet the text does not necessarily suggest immorality. The woman may have had five husbands for a variety of reasons. She was not necessarily divorced; her husbands may have died. She may have been caught up in a levirate marriage that required the brothers of a deceased husband to marry her. The last male in line may have refused to marry her, so that he is not now her husband.

The focus is upon the unnamed foreign woman's recognizing—in stages—who Christ is. She knows him as she comes to realize that he knows her. (She is surprised, never ashamed.) At first she sees him as a Jew (4:9), then she calls him "Sir" (4:11). Next she compares him with the great ancestor Jacob (4:12). Once she experiences herself as known by him, she identifies him as a prophet (4:19). Finally, she wonders, *He cannot be the Messiah, can he?* (4:29).

Besides the theme of being known and knowing, crossing boundaries is a prominent theme of this encounter. Before this trip to Samaria, Jesus' ministry had centered upon the places of official Judaism. Here he meets a person outside this official domain and immediately crosses the boundary between the Jews and Samaritans—a boundary maintained by fierce rivalry for several centuries. (The Samaritans had built a shrine on Mount Gerizim rather than focusing their worship in Jerusalem. The Jews destroyed that shrine in 128 B.C.E.)

At the time of Jesus, a Jew should not even have talked to a Samaritan, let alone drink water from a Samaritan vessel. A rabbi was not to talk with a woman in public anywhere, but Jesus engages her in serious theological discussion and does not waiver when his disciples arrive, perplexed.

Jesus shatters the status quo, the social conventions based on gender, and even the idea that there is a chosen people and a rejected people: He wants it to be known that God offers grace for all!

To a woman who regularly walks a good distance to get water for her family—and many women around the world still do this today—this message of living water is liberation indeed.

FOR YOUR MEDITATION: Because this woman courageously engaged Jesus in serious theological conversation, this meditation is an excellent opportunity for posing your contemporary theological questions to your "image" of Jesus.

While any group or individual could benefit from encountering "images" of Jesus or the unnamed woman, this meditation lends itself to settings in which some people present may identify with the Samaritans, some with the Jews, some with males, some with females.

This meditation is prepared for you to take on the identity of the unnamed woman. If you prefer, you may observe that woman, rather than imagining yourself in her place.

MEDITATION: Stretch your arms and legs, your torso; become comfortable in your posture and take a few deep breaths. In your mind's eye, find a place that means a good deal to you: a place of your ancestors, a place of worship, or a place where you find nourishment. Let yourself be alone in this place. Experience yourself there, alone, yet aware of "your people."

Now the Christ enters into this place. The Christ asks you for some particular thing that you are able to give. . . . What is your reaction? Let yourself and the Christ interact. . . . The Christ clearly knows you, even your past. . . . How do you respond? Be open to grasping new insights. . . .

Ask the Christ questions you have been pondering. . . . Hear the responses. . . . Dialogue as long as you want.

Now others arrive, surprised to see you talking. . . . What is your reaction?

Go to tell whomever you want about your encounter. . . . As you tell these people of your encounter with Christ, notice your thoughts and feelings as they react to you.

Now return to the site of your encounter with the Christ. Stay there as long as you need to, then affirm amen.

COMMENTS ON DEBRIEFING AND USE: Clay would be a marvelous medium to debrief this meditation—clay with a lot of water too. Sculpt the place, the request of Christ from you, the image of yourself, the image of Christ, or the people to whom you go to share your convictions.

Compare the views you held of the unnamed biblical woman before the meditation with the thoughts and feelings you have about her after this meditation. If you are in a group, hear how others experienced being the unnamed woman in their imagination. Whether you are male or female, imagine this entire encounter again, but this time imagine being an unnamed male whom Jesus meets at the well.

14

THE FOUNDATION OF YOUR HOME

READING: "Why do you call me 'Lord, Lord,' and do not do what I tell you? I will show you what someone is like who comes to me, hears my words, and acts on them. That one is like a man building a house, who dug deeply and laid the foundation on rock; when a flood arose, the river burst against that house but could not shake it, because it had been well built. But the one who hears and does not act is like a man who built a house on the ground without a foundation. When the river burst against it, immediately it fell, and great was the ruin of that house" (Luke 6:46-49; see also Matthew 7:24-28).

BIBLICAL NOTE: In Luke's version, both men build their houses on the ground, the soil. What differentiates them is whether or not the builder put energy into laying a sturdy foundation, digging deep into the soil to have a foundation of rock. Matthew's narrative emphasizes the difference in the choice of locations for the houses—sand or rock.

FOR YOUR MEDITATION: Jesus refers to the builder as constructing a house; this meditation focuses upon your home. You could alter the meditation to refer to your church, school, community, work environment, or even your nation. A family of more than one can practice this meditation together, then share with one another. A community or church event could include this meditation with group reflection.

Think first of some qualities or values that are important to you in the setting you have chosen.

MEDITATION: Take a few slow, deep breaths and relax. Visualize yourself in some comfortable part of your home. . . . As you get a sense of yourself there, get in touch with some qualities or values you would like to have expressed in your home. Reflect on these as long as you choose. . . . Now slowly walk around your home in your imagination, aware of the

90

feelings you have as you go from room to room. . . . Do this in much detail, perhaps picking up things around your house as you walk, perhaps talking to family members as you move from room to room. . . . Experience each room in your home. . . .

Now stop in a place of your own choosing. . . . Recall the feelings you had as you moved around your home. . . . Pay attention to any images, ideas, or feelings that arise. . . . Now think of a quality or value that is important to you. . . . Walk around your home again in your imagination, seeing the rooms filled with stronger expressions of this value or quality. The house is being shored up with this quality or value. Notice any changes that occur. . . .

Now imagine a storm's hitting your home. . . . It may be a physical storm or a storm of emotions or events. . . . Observe how your home endures the storm. . . . Bring in any assistance you need for repairing or rebuilding, even to rebuild the foundation. . . .

When the home is rebuilt, look around for evidence of the quality or value you cherish. . . . Maintain calm for a while. . . . Know that you can return to this image of your home whenever you choose. When you feel ready, open your eyes.

COMMENTS ON DEBRIEFING AND USE: Draw four pictures of your home: how it looked at first, how it appeared with the values or qualities strengthened, how it looked after the storm, and finally how it changed with any repairs. This activity could lead to further discussion about each of the stages. When used in a group, adequate debriefing of this meditation takes at least an hour.

15

BLOOMING

READING:
> The wilderness and the dry
>   land shall be glad,
>   the desert shall rejoice and blossom;
>   like the crocus it shall blossom abundantly,
>   and rejoice with joy and singing (Isaiah 35: 1-2).

BIBLICAL NOTE: Isaiah 34 speaks of the nations' destruction, their culture turned to wasteland because of God's judgment. The people had placed their hope only in human power. Now in Isaiah 35, we see another appearance of God—this time to make a fertile oasis out of the desert wasteland and to refashion the salvation road that humans can learn to walk. Salvation and re-creation are possible! Radical reversals for humanity and for creation itself can occur.

FOR YOUR MEDITATION: This passage conveys a profound theological belief that God offers individuals and societies opportunities for new life again and again. We cannot eliminate the past (individual mistakes, societal wars, or planetary waste and pollution), but we can make a radical reversal.

You might want to choose this meditation when you are in a "wilderness" or "dry place" in your life. Or you may practice this meditation simply to become more aware of life blooming through you.

A group of about a dozen ministers—local church pastors, chaplains, educators, and counselors—shared this meditation at a monthly gathering, and found themselves refreshed in their ministries.[6]

MEDITATION: Become quiet, close your eyes, and take a few, slow, deep breaths. . . . Imagine yourself in a meadow. Feel how tall the grass is; feel it against your legs. . . . Experience yourself walking through this meadow. . . . Look around you to see what else is there. . . . Notice the fragrance of the grass, trees, and flowers, or whatever is there. . . . Observe whether the meadow is sloping or flat. . . . Notice the colors. . . . Feel the warmth of the sun radiating down upon you and warming up the whole meadow. . . . Now you walk to the edge of the meadow and discover a desert. Stand there for a while and become aware of what you experience, observing that apparently barren area. . . .

Enter into the desert. Experience being in the desert. . . . Take time to explore it, to wander in it. Feel yourself being there. [*long pause*] Now, before your eyes, the desert blooms. . . . See it bloom. . . . Become aware of your feelings as you see the desert bloom around you. . . . Notice the colors, the fragrances, the sounds. . . . Allow yourself to feel a part of this blooming. . . . Reach out to pick up some symbol that represents this blooming desert.

Make your way back to the meadow at your own pace, in your own way. . . . When you get back to the meadow, look around and observe the meadow again. . . . Remember the symbol that you brought back from the desert. When you feel ready, open your eyes.

COMMENTS ON DEBRIEFING AND USE: First draw the meadow, then the desert, then the desert in bloom. Ask yourself, "What part of my life is like the desert?" Notice the connections between your life and the images in the meditation. If you practice this in a group, ask "What aspect of your group life is like a barren desert, like a desert in bloom?"

16

CELEBRATING SEXUALITY

READING:

> The Song of Songs, which is Solomon's.
> Let him kiss me with the kisses of
>   his mouth! (1:1-2)

> The flowers appear on the earth;
>   the time of singing has come,
> and the voice of the turtledove
>   is heard in our land.
> The fig tree puts forth its figs,
>   and the vines are in blossom;
>   they give forth fragrance.
> Arise, my love, my fair one,
>   and come away (Song of Solomon 2:12-13).

BIBLICAL NOTE: This anthology of twenty-five to thirty separate love poems were possibly oral works, composed for use at weddings. In Hebrew *Song of Songs* is stated in the superlative, meaning something like "The Greatest Song." It celebrates the many aspects of love: courtship, fantasies, secret encounters, physical sexuality, and reminders to be patient, to seek guidance in love matters. Female and male voices exchange love poems; perhaps it is a chorus that comments and reflects.

Commentators for centuries have given an allegorical meaning to this poetry by likening the love between the man and woman to that of God and Israel or Christ and the church. Tom Dozeman points out that in ancient Israel, secular poetry did not exist. Frequently God and sexuality were combined in the ancient Near East,[7] as in other ancient religions. If we stress the potential allegorical meaning too much, we lose the power of the celebration of human sexuality—a major purpose of these songs.

FOR YOUR MEDITATION: You may want to read all of The Song of Songs to reflect upon the vast array of possibilities in relationships. Some people are reluctant to think about or talk about their sexuality in a sacred context—how far we have come from ancient times! The reluctance of some need not veto others from making connections between their spirituality and sexuality, but it is wise to attend to the various attitudes from the start.

Clearly couples may appreciate this meditation as they make decisions about their relationships, celebrate anniversaries, cherish memories, or revive their feelings of love.

MEDITATION: Become aware of your body; relax and enjoy being in your body. Take some deep breaths, noticing the feeling of the air as it moves in and slowly out of your body. Stretch your arms and legs. Experience your bodiliness.

Imagine being in a grassy meadow. . . . Sense yourself in the warm light of the Sacred. God's warmth, love, and the light of wisdom surround your body and immerse it.

You look around and realize that flowers are appearing—it is spring. . . . Take time to observe the various buds, blossoms, vines, trees, and flowers around you. Notice fragrances too. . . . Pay attention to the colors. Observe small details and the large scene. . . . Now pay attention to the sounds: cooing of turtledoves, chirping or warbling of birds, buzzing sounds—the many sounds of spring.

Now be aware of the one whom you love and who loves you, either with you or entering the meadow. Express your love to each other. Sense the beauty, the color, the vitality of spring in your relationship. Communicate as you desire. . . .

When you are ready, say good-bye to this meadow, going away together. Sit in silence, then affirm amen.

COMMENTS ON DEBRIEFING AND USE: In a group, it is important to let people share only as they choose. With this particular meditation, it helps to have people write first in their own journals—whether journals they keep regularly or special ones for the occasion.

Even couples who have been together many years are sometimes reluctant to talk to each other about their sexuality, especially mixed with prayer. However, sharing images, feelings, and hopes with each other can be precious, intimate sharing.

17

One Body—Many Integral Parts

Reading: For just as the body is one and has many members, and all the members of the body, though many, are one body, so it is with Christ. For in the one Spirit we were all baptized into one body—Jews or Greeks, slaves or free—and we were all made to drink of one Spirit.

Indeed, the body does not consist of one member but of many. If the foot would say, "Because I am not a hand, I do not belong to the body," that would not make it any less a part of the body. And if the ear would say, "Because I am not an eye, I do not belong to the body," that would not make it any less a part of the body. And if the ear would say, "Because I am not an eye, I do not belong to the body," that would not make it any less a part of the body. If the whole body were an eye, where would the hearing be? If the whole body were hearing, where would the sense of smell be? But as it is, God arranged the members in the body. . . . The eye cannot say to the hand, "I have no need of you," nor again the head to the feet, "I have no need of you.". . . If one member suffers, all suffer together with it; if one member is honored, all rejoice together with it (1 Corinthians 12:12-18, 21, 26).

Biblical Note: This image is a splendid metaphor for an ethnically and socially inclusive church. Every part is important.

In Paul's day, philosophers spoke of the cosmos as a body with complementary elements, using the body metaphor. But Paul's letter gives this image a twist, for now the body is the body of Christ, the church. Sallie McFague proposes another shift that would be ecologically as well as theologically sound. We can consider the universe or world as God's body, a body enlivened and empowered by the divine Spirit.[8]

For Your Meditation: This meditation has two parts. The first part encourages you to pay attention to your body, to relax and cherish it. The second relates to a body of persons in which you participate. You may practice both together, or you may choose to practice each one separately—as the occasion or situation seems appropriate.

This passage from First Corinthians profoundly affirms the ministry of the laity. This meditation would be appropriate for churches when they honor the service of members, install officers, welcome new members, or celebrate baptisms or confirmations. It could be considered for World Communion Sunday or on days when the church focuses attention on ethnic or social diversity or ecumenical Christian events. This meditation also has an ecological dimension—one person's suffering or rejoicing affects all other members. You could use this meditation at any event that lifts up the importance of the earth and our relationship with it.

Families can benefit from this meditation too as persons become aware of the gifts and roles of family members. Blended families, which connect parents, stepparents, siblings, stepsiblings, and even grandparents could discuss their newly formed family in the midst of this prayer.

MEDITATION A: Sit quietly. Let yourself relax, taking a few deep breaths. . . . Become aware of your feet. Tense them, then let them relax. . . . Focus on your calves; tense them, then relax. . . . Let your thighs tense, then relax. . . . Feel your legs tense, then relax, letting go. . . . Tense, then relax your lower abdomen. . . . Feel your stomach tensing, then relaxing. . . . Let a large breath flow through you and feel your chest cavity relax. . . . Feel your upper arms tense, then relax. . . . Tense your wrists, hands, and lower arms, then relax them all. . . . Tense your neck muscles gently; let them relax. . . . Let a sense of relaxation radiate from the center of your forehead throughout your face. Feel your cheek muscles relax. . . . Relax your jaw. . . . Feel your tongue relaxing and your throat. . . . Relax your scalp. . . . Go back through your body, exploring to find any tight spots; let them relax. . . .

MEDITATION B: Become aware of your feet; focus your awareness on your feet. Move your feet and focus your attention on your feet. . . . Become aware of your whole body's response to the movement of your feet. Stop moving your feet; feel your body's response. Now direct your attention to your stomach. Move your stomach around from within . . . Get a sense of your body as a whole, responding to the movement of your stomach. Continue to do this with various parts of your body, putting your attention at the one point, focusing your awareness there, then moving your attention to an awareness of your whole body's response to the part.

97

Now reflect on a community to which you belong. . . . Become aware of yourself within that community. . . . Think of yourself and the role that you play in this community. . . . Consider your responsibility, your functions, your gifts. . . . Now become aware of the whole community's response to you—to your role and gifts.

Move your awareness to another person within this community. . . . What is that person's role and function within the community? Now sense the relationship between that person and the community.

Identify some joy in another person; experience how that affects you. . . . Become aware of some joy within yourself; experience how that affects the other person. . . . Reflect on some sorrow or pain within that person. . . . Become aware of the effect of that sorrow on you. . . . Likewise, remember some pain in your own life. . . . Get some sense of how that affects the other one. . . .

If someone within this community is estranged from others so that he or she might feel the others believe *We have no need of you*, focus on that person. Imagine the relationship of that one and the others, how they need one another. Shift to another person. . . . Notice the interconnections. See how the persons, including yourself, rejoice in one another's blessings and repond to one another's hurts..

When you feel finished, become aware of yourself, your gift to this community, your function. Now become aware of your own physical body again—your whole body and its many parts. . . . When you are ready, open your eyes.

COMMENTS ON DEBRIEFING AND USE: As you talk with others, you may discover not only their perceptions of your role and behavior but also a level of concern that surprises you. Accept whatever occurs as present perceptions. Each member of a group has a different perspective.

Even though each person's roles and functions are important and valued, those can change if someone realizes that certain roles or functions limit an individual or the group as a whole. This meditation may help some members choose to expand the use of their abilities!

If you practice this meditation in a group, draw diagrams, which represent your gifts and roles as you and others see them. It is fun to compare the diagrams. One person may see another as a peacemaker, while that one sees herself or himself as a troublemaker. Look at the various diagrams, affirm one another, and reflect upon desired changes.

18

WISDOM'S CALL

Does not wisdom call,
and does not understanding raise her voice?
On the heights, beside the way,
    at the crossroads she takes her stand;
beside the gates in front of the town,
    at the entrance of the portals she cries out:
"To you, O people, I call,
    and my cry is to all that live.
O simple ones, learn prudence;
    acquire intelligence, you who lack it.
Hear, for I will speak noble things,
    and from my lips will come what is right;
for my mouth will utter truth;
    wickedness is an abomination to my lips.

. . . .

I have good advice and sound wisdom;
I have insight, I have strength" (Proverbs 8:1-7, 14).

BIBLICAL NOTE: In Proverbs 8, Wisdom talks directly to humans twice, in vv. 4-11 and 32-36. Between these addresses, she identifies herself: God gave birth to her (verse 22). She explains that God shaped the mountains, firmed up the skies, limited the seas—that is, God crafted out of chaos the earth as we know it. But she was begotten, not made—birthed, not crafted. She has authority in part because of her birth by God, but also because she, witnessing the rest of creation, knows the mysteries that are part of the fabric of creation. No one else does. So her teachings are certainly worth heeding.[9]

In the Hebrew Scriptures, Wisdom seeks out followers. She is available. She even advertises what she has to offer and wants people to pay attention. We see her raising her voice "on the heights, beside the way, at the crossroads," and "beside the gates in front of the town." She takes her stand and cries out to be heard. Wisdom is part of the everydayness of life; what she offers is relevant and practical. If humans do not follow her accessible guidance, they are refusing to listen by their own choosing.

Given this strong Wisdom tradition in Judaism, it is understandable that some early Christians identified Jesus with Wisdom. He too was said to be a begotten child of God; he too had very earthly advice that he wanted others to follow.

FOR YOUR MEDITATION: By personifying wisdom, the poet engages us, the hearer. But we are unclear as to what Wisdom actually represents in this passage. Is Wisdom a characteristic of God's creative activity? a companion with a distinct identity? an originally independent divine being? a figure of speech, standing for the collective traditions of the wise?[10] These are fascinating questions for biblical study and theological discussion. For us, as we meditate, it matters little. Wisdom may emerge in our imaginations as any of these representations.

MEDITATION: If possible, stretch your arms, legs, and torso. Relax your shoulders, stomach, neck, and eyes. Become comfortable and breathe slowly and deeply a few times. . . . Imagine yourself. Just get a sense of yourself as you are. . . . Envision sunshine pouring over you, warming you, so that you are touched by light, warmth, and love. . . . Now imagine yourself in some setting in which you desire greater wisdom.

As you are in this setting, you see a crossroads. . . . You look, then realize that Wisdom is taking a stand at that very crossroads. . . . Notice what the crossroads are and interact with Wisdom in whatever way seems right. . . . Try to discover what is being recommended. . . . If you want to bring in any other person or symbol, do that. Let Wisdom share with you and whatever or whomever you bring in.

You look in another direction and see a gate . . . an entrance. . . . Wisdom is there, crying out to you to hear truth. Take time to get a sense of Wisdom, to hear what is being said. Do what you need to in order to understand. Try to name the gate. To what is it the entrance?

You hear Wisdom say, "I have insight, I have strength." Sense what that might be for you. Do what you need to do to gain some of that strength and insight. A symbol of Wisdom's guidance may appear for you. Accept it. Now bid Wisdom farewell, knowing that you can return to

Wisdom as you choose. When you feel ready, declare amen, and open your eyes.

COMMENTS ON DEBRIEFING AND USE: Draw the crossroads, the gates, and how you pictured Wisdom. If you are feeling particularly playful, use pipe cleaners to create a mixed-media collage. Write some of the insights you have gained or questions you now have.

19

BLESSED IS THE CHILD

READING: People were bringing little children to him in order that he might touch them; and the disciples spoke sternly to them. But when Jesus saw this, he was indignant and said to them, "Let the little children come to me; do not stop them; for it is to such as these that the kingdom of God belongs. Truly I tell you, whoever does not receive the kingdom of God as a little child will never enter it." And he took them up in his arms, laid his hands on them, and blessed them (Mark 10:13-16; see also Matthew 19:13-15; Luke 18:15-17).

BIBLICAL NOTE: Commentators give this passage little attention. Often preachers assume that Jesus commends the childlike values of trust or joy. However, we must view this passage within the context of Jesus' entire message. Jesus turns over the existing hierarchies: The rich have a hard time getting into the kingdom, while the poor are ready; the pious need to search themselves to see what they are willing to give up, while those who know themselves to be sinners hear the good news of God's grace; those with power over others have to relinquish their belief in their own superiority, accepting all others as equal.

Children were considered property. They were seen as unequal, the lowest in the family hierarchy. Jesus is preaching his gospel message one more time: We enter the reign (*kin*dom) of God when we do not imagine value distinctions between people. The child is blessed because we all are blessed as children of God. *We never have to become "better than" children.*

FOR YOUR MEDITATION: Use this meditation on the many occasions that focus on children. However, the message is truly an adult one. We adults need to give up our presumptuousness of being better than, more spiritual than children. While retaining appropriate authority, we should see in children their own authority under God, which requires our respect.

MEDITATION: Take a few deep breaths, letting yourself sink down, to be supported. Let the floor, chair, whatever you are sitting on, hold you up. . . . Give it your weight.

Imagine a large crowd. . . . The setting may be a familiar one or one that you have never seen before. See people of different ages, conditions, and economic situations. Notice evidence of different religious beliefs and various ethnic backgrounds. . . . Notice how you feel as you walk around in this crowd, as you observe. . . . Pay attention to any judgments that you make as you look. Which persons have more worth? less worth?

Now you meet the Christ. The Christ points out some children, saying, "Whoever does not receive the kingdom of God as a little child will never enter it." How do you respond? . . . Talk with the Christ about your views of the people around you. . . . Continue the dialogue as long as you need. Bid farewell to the Christ when you choose. Notice again your feelings as you are in the midst of this crowd. When you are ready, affirm amen.

COMMENTS ON DEBRIEFING AND USE: There are many pictures of Jesus with children. It may be evocative to surround a room with these pictures while practicing this meditation. The meditation may trouble some adults. Many have thought of this passage as playful (I emphasized the "child within" for this meditation in the first edition of *Opening to God*). However, this passage is really quite sobering. It causes us to question how we think of equality, how we cherish our attachment of value in some people over that of others. An honest self-appraisal or discussion between those of each gender and several races could be enlightening. Who do we really consider godlike? closer to God? ungodlike? further from God?

20

BEFRIENDING MARTHA AND MARY

READING: Now as they went on their way, he entered a certain village, where a woman named Martha welcomed him into her home. She had a sister named Mary, who sat at the Lord's feet and listened to what he was saying. But Martha was distracted by her many tasks; so she came to him and asked, "Lord, do you not care that my sister has left me to do all the work by myself? Tell her then to help me." But the Lord answered her, "Martha, Martha, you are worried and distracted by many things; there is need of only one thing. Mary has chosen the better part, which will not be taken away from her" (Luke 10:38-42).

BIBLICAL NOTE: Jesus comes with his disciples to a village where Martha welcomes him to her home. Mary, Martha's sister, is present, perhaps along with other disciples.

Mary is silent throughout—while listening to Jesus and while hearing her sister's frustration as she receives no help from Mary. Martha asks, "Lord, don't you care that my sister has left me to serve alone? Tell her then to help me." Professor Jane Schaberg points out that this request for help is similar to that made by the disciples in the boat that was sinking: "Teacher, do you not care that we are perishing?"(Mark 4:38). In that incident, Jesus calmed the storm. Here he gently chides Martha, leaving the situation as it is. Martha is now silenced—her request denied.[11]

Do not feel alone if you find this passage perplexing; few agree about its meaning! In the first edition of *Opening to God*, I portrayed Martha and Mary as representing responsibilities or chores versus spiritual matters. People have tried to represent the two women as models of active or contemplative lifestyles or as examples of female career choices. But these portrayals are not in the text itself. Elizabeth Schüssler Fiorenza suggests that Luke is making a distinction between different types of offices in the first-century church, as well as discussing the role of women in those churches.[12]

FOR YOUR MEDITATION: I know of no woman who does not react viscerally to this passage. (As men are more aware of their own domestic responsibilities and choices, men too may react more strongly to this passage.) The "meaning" of Jesus' words is open to interpretation (in light of Luke's own intentions). Allow this meditation to be a springboard for a discussion or inner reflection.

In their debriefing, many people comment that Martha was preparing a meal. It is fascinating to notice that the scripture passage itself does not mention a meal! This small matter helps us see how we project our own expectations, what we have heard in sermons or our preconceived ideas about what women do, onto the passage.

Even though this passage is of great relevance to women, men can benefit from observing and identifying with the biblical characters. This meditation should not be limited to groups of women or women's individual practice. Consider using it as an opening prayer for participants in a men's group that is reflecting upon gender-based assumptions.

MEDITATION: Become quiet; take a few deep, slow breaths as you let go of concerns or tensions. . . . Simply be quiet. . . . Now visualize a home. See how it is built and furnished. Notice any colors, fragrances, or sounds in the home. You see now two women and perhaps other people. Martha is there and Mary; then the Christ enters. . . . Notice that Mary is now listening to the Christ speak. . . . Martha is involved in other tasks. . . . Notice what Martha does. After a while she becomes impatient, wanting help. . . . She speaks to the Christ, asking, "Shouldn't Mary be helping me?" Allow the Christ to answer. . . . Let Mary, Martha, and the Christ interact. . . . You might experience yourself being each of these three people. . . . Continue the interaction until you arrive at some resolution or you are aware that there is no resolution. . . . Become aware of your feelings and thoughts, the possible feelings and thoughts of each person. . . . Knowing that you can return to this home in your imagination, bid farewell to Martha, Mary, and the Christ. When you are ready, open your eyes.

COMMENTS ON DEBRIEFING AND USE: Draw Martha, Mary, the Christ, and any additional people who were in the scene of your meditation. In word balloons (found in cartoon speech), write the most dramatic words each exchanged. (I recall one exciting group session in which Jesus got up and helped Martha, so that all could talk together.)

List the feelings you experienced while you identified with any of the three persons. Consider how these relate to your current life situation. In a discussion with others or after personal reflection, discern whether you need to make any changes in the way you interact with others. Notice whether you have been bound by any gender stereotypes or pulled into competition with others when you did not want to. Observe whether you need to take concrete action.

21

Rekindling the Faith of Our Forebears

Reading: I am grateful to God—whom I worship with a clear conscience, as my ancestors did—when I remember you constantly in my prayers night and day. Recalling your tears, I long to see you so that I may be filled with joy. I am reminded of your sincere faith, a faith that lived first in your grandmother Lois and your mother Eunice and now, I am sure, lives in you. For this reason I remind you to rekindle the gift of God that is within you through the laying on of my hands; for God did not give us a spirit of cowardice, but rather a spirit of power and of love and of self-discipline (2 Timothy 1:3-7).

Biblical Note: Timothy was from Lystra (in Asia Minor), the son of a Greek father and a Jewish mother who had become Christian (Acts 16:1). We learn in 2 Timothy 1:5 and 3:15 that Timothy, who had learned the Hebrew Scriptures as a child, had become a Christian before Paul's arrival, due to the influence of his mother Eunice and his grandmother Lois.

Timothy seems to have been a companion and fellow worker of Paul—a younger colleague. Scripture presents him as shy, perhaps fearful of declaring his own authority. Paul encourages him to be brave in the midst of persecution, to rekindle the authority that Paul had laid upon him, and to remember the heritage of his faith, which lives in him.

For Your Meditation: Before meditating, list influences upon your current faith. List parents, grandparents, and extended family who influenced you. Add the names of teachers, neighbors, even TV personalities who affected your faith. Remember places of worship, books read, stories narrated. Allow yourself to reminisce upon the heritage of your current faith, making notes as you recall even more influences upon you.

For this meditation, the letter may be from someone living currently in your life. It can, however, be from someone who has died but from whose spirit you can receive encouragement or guidance.

MEDITATION: Get into a comfortable posture, free from distractions. Rock gently back and forth a few times, then find the position in which you are centered. Bracket any concerns for a few minutes, just lay them aside. Take several slow, deep breaths, inhaling fresh revitalizing air and exhaling any worries or tensions along with the air. . . .

Imagine yourself in a comfortable spot in your home or in some other location. Look around, listen, sense what it is like to be there. . . . A letter arrives. You open this letter, which is addressed to you, and read it. It is from a friend. Notice your experience as you receive, open this letter, and realize who it is from. Now read the beginning of the letter.

The one who wrote this letter encourages you to remember those who helped you on your faith journey . . . to rekindle your courage and faith by thinking of them and their influences. . . . Allow to come to mind various people who encouraged your faith. . . . You may engage in dialogue with any of them, asking questions or sharing with them now. . . . Take as long as you need, interacting with several of those who influenced and encouraged you. Pick up the letter again. In some way it encourages you to take authority in your current situation. Imagine what it would be like to take appropriate authority in your current situation. . . . Get a sense of yourself with appropriate authority.

Now look at the letter once more. When you are ready, fold the letter and put it away in a place where you can retrieve it again. Become aware of your surroundings and open your eyes.

COMMENTS ON DEBRIEFING AND USE: Making this imagery prayer concrete may take several forms: (1) Make a timeline, naming those who influenced your faith, labeling the gifts they gave you by their names. (2) In the middle of a piece of paper, write a word or two that describes yourself or situation today or a quality that you would like to develop (such as courage). Then, as spokes to a wheel, write the names of those who have influenced you or continue to encourage you. (3) Write a letter to yourself as if someone important to you had written it, saying what you think he or she would say or what you would like to hear. 4) Write a letter to someone to encourage *him* or *her* in the faith journey; mail it!

22

AT LEAST THREE CHOICES
IN RISKY SITUATIONS

[The BIBLICAL NOTE introduces the passage.]

BIBLICAL NOTE: Esther is a marvelous book in Hebrew Scriptures, one of the five "little books" that are read on various feast days in the Jewish tradition. Esther is read during the festival of Purim, a two-day celebration in what corresponds to February-March. A primary message of the book is this: We don't know exactly how God is acting in a situation; we're not always sure what we are being called to do. We have to pay attention to our own consciences, seek counsel from trusted friends, and act despite our unsurety of the consequences.

In the midst of King Ahasuerus's rule over Persia in the year 470 B.C.E., he gave a lavish banquet that lasted 180 days. When he decided to show off Queen Vashti to those at the party, she refused! She said no. For this, she was deposed.

The king searched for another queen, finding Esther (who, unknown to him, was a Jew), whom he favored. She had been an orphan—Mordecai, her uncle, had adopted and raised her. Haman held a high position in the Persian government, so others bowed down to him. However, Mordecai would not bow to anyone but God. Haman plotted to destroy Mordecai; he managed to get the king to sign a decree that all the Jews be destroyed one year hence. Mordecai discovered this plot and presented it to Esther, asking her to do something to save her people. (The king and Haman were unaware that Mordecai was related to the queen.) It is at this point that we come to the famous words of Mordecai, "Who knows? Perhaps you have come to royal dignity for just such a time as this."

After praying, Esther decides to invite the king and Haman to a two-day festival in her house. It is risky for her even to approach the king, without his requesting her. But on the second day of the festival, she gathers courage to ask the king to spare her people. Since the king cannot withdraw the first decree, he supplements it with another decree: The Jews may defend themselves.

The Jews do defend themselves, killing 75,000 of their "enemy." Not only that, but Haman hangs on the gallows he had built for Mordecai.

READING: But Queen Vashti refused to come at the king's command conveyed by the eunuchs. At this the king was enraged, and his anger burned within him. . . .

When they told Mordecai what Esther had said, Mordecai told them to reply to Esther, "Do not think that in the king's palace you will escape any more than all the other Jews. For if you keep silence at such a time as this, relief and deliverance will rise for the Jews from another quarter, but you and your father's family will perish. Who knows? Perhaps you have come to royal dignity for just such a time as this" (Esther 1:12; 4:12-14).

FOR YOUR MEDITATION: When reading this book, it is tempting to focus exclusively upon Queen Esther who said yes to a request made upon her—to save her people. We also need to remember Queen Vashti who said no to a request made upon her. Sometimes we accidentally take any request made of us as a call by God! We elevate the answer yes without realizing that no can be guidance suggested by God also.

I have found much value in a "three-choice" exercise, which we can practice in the midst of our daily decisions. At times we feel stuck, as if we "have to say yes." Other times, we feel pressured to decide yes or no. But in *many* circumstances, we have at least three choices. We do not need to allow ourselves to feel limited by one or two options. We can think to ourselves, *What are three options for my response?* Or together with those making a decision, *What are three choices we could make?* When we challenge ourselves to come up with three ideas, usually even more than three emerge. These options free us to be more creative and to feel less cornered by the situation.[13]

Because Vashti said no, which was a risk; and Esther said yes, which was also risky, these two women represent courageous options in choice making to me. This meditation will not follow the biblical story but will call on these women, in imagination, as wisdom figures, to offer guidance today. They may be represented by people you actually know; they may be themselves as they appear in scripture, or you may visualize completely imaginary people in your meditation.

MEDITATION: If possible, move around a bit, getting a sense of your body. Feel free to dance or to stretch. Laugh, cry, cough, growl—whatever is appropriate for your situation, emotions, and body. . . . Now gather yourself to a comfortable position and take a few deep, slow breaths. Let yourself relax.

Imagine yourself in a nurturing setting—one in which you are open, receptive, and creative. Perhaps this is a grassy area, an area of trees, a sacred place, or a home. Move around in your imagination until you find a safe, creative, nurturing place. . . . Now focus on the smells, sights, sounds, even tastes of this place. . . .

Allow a situation in which you need to make a decision to come to your mind. Focus on that decision. Perhaps someone has asked you to do something. You are deciding how to respond. Perhaps a situation in your life calls for action on your part; you have to decide how to act.

Invite Queen Vashti, Queen Esther, and anyone else you choose into your imagination—wise people from the Bible or wise people you know. Tell these wise people your predicament and let them respond. . . . Think of at least three choices that you could make. . . . Let others help you. . . . Take as long as you need.

If you need to inquire about options or to create other scenes in your imagination, go ahead; do that. . . .

Notice whether you have arrived at a decision for action. Remember the other choices you could have made. If you have not yet decided, accept the fact that now you are undecided. When you feel ready, say good-bye to your wise people, thanking them, then affirm amen.

COMMENTS ON DEBRIEFING AND USE: Definitely write down the situation and the three (or more) choices that are possible for you to make at this time. You may want to continue your reflection, writing pros and cons, feelings, or consequences to each of these choices. You could act out being Vashti, saying no and Esther, saying yes. Act out other wise people, getting a sense of their power to make good decisions. Then become yourself again. Try on the different decisions to see how they fit.

23

1/28 N

THE VINEDRESSER, THE VINE, AND THE VINEYARD

READING: "I am the true vine, and my Father is the vinegrower. He removes every branch in me that bears no fruit. Every branch that bears fruit he prunes to make it bear more fruit. You have already been cleansed by the word that I have spoken to you. Abide in me as I abide in you. Just as the branch cannot bear fruit by itself unless it abides in the vine, neither can you unless you abide in me. I am the vine, you are the branches. Those who abide in me and I in them bear much fruit, because apart from me you can do nothing (John 15:1-5).

BIBLICAL NOTE: The Gospel of John records this and several other "I am" speeches delivered by Jesus. All these speeches remind us of God's answer to Moses when Moses asked God who he should say sent him. God answered, "I AM."

The metaphor moves from Christ as the vine; to God as the vinedresser; to the branches, the believers who are living according to Christ.

FOR YOUR MEDITATION: This meditation is similar to Meditation 4, "Reflections upon Your Seeds," in that you reflect on aspects of your life that are barren or do not take root and other aspects that flourish. (Remember the barren images offer guidance just as the flourishing ones do.) You may want to use these meditations in tandem, during a retreat, or one at the beginning and one at the end of a course of study.

You could list all the "I am" statements of Christ, meditating upon each one, over a period of time.[14]

MEDITATION: Take a few deep breaths. . . . Get a sense of yourself in some grassy area. . . . It might be a meadow or a garden. . . . Be aware of your feelings being there. . . . Look all around you to see what is there.

Notice any people or vegetation. . . . Now become aware of the grass—how high it is, the color, the fragrances. . . . Let yourself feel the warmth of the sun radiating down upon you and the whole area.

Now walk until you find a vine, a beautiful vine. . . . Notice the branches, how they intertwine. . . . Notice the fruit, the blossoms, the colors. . . . Observe some of the twigs that look as though they are just about dead . . . the twigs that need to be broken off. . . . Now become aware of someone who is in charge of this garden and this vine . . . a Gardener. The Gardener takes care of the vine, takes care of each of the branches. . . . Stay in touch with this caring and the love of the Gardener.

Notice a barren branch, something that needs to be trimmed away. Think of something in your life that needs to be trimmed. Imagine its being trimmed away.

Look for a branch that has fruit yet needs a slight pruning. . . . Allow something in your life to come to mind that needs pruning. Imagine its being pruned. . . . You may ask for any help you need. . . .

Now look for a fruitful branch. . . . Let something in your life that is fruitful come to your mind. . . . Observe that; get a sense of the life of the vine moving through that fruit. . . . Celebrate, enjoy that fruitfulness. . . . Let yourself experience it with satisfaction.

Think back over the three things that emerged for you: something barren, something to be pruned, something very fruitful. . . . Take a look at this garden. . . . Sense the warmth, the life flowing through it, the care within it, the love of the Gardener. . . . Become aware of your breathing and the room in which you are sitting. When you are ready, open your eyes.

COMMENTS ON DEBRIEFING AND USE: This visual imagery begs to be drawn! Consider making a mural, using long, large paper and drawing with many bold-colored markers and earthy crayons. If time allows, create papier-maché leaves and branches. Or glue branches and leaves made from construction paper to the mural. Consider how to image the Gardener.

A group of persons could draw on the same mural, allowing their individual branches to intertwine one with another.

Grape juice or wine would be a fitting beverage to serve as you debrief. Consider hosting a love feast or eucharistic meal.

24

FEELING FORSAKEN

READING: From noon on, darkness came over the whole land until three in the afternoon. And about three o'clock Jesus cried with a loud voice, "Eli, Eli, lema sabachthani?" that is, "My God, my God, why have you forsaken me?" (Matthew 27:45-46).

BIBLICAL NOTE: We usually recall these words from Jesus on Good Friday, for he utters them from the cross. Jesus is reciting Psalm 22, a psalm of lament that expresses loneliness and bewilderment yet ends with hope.

FOR YOUR MEDITATION: In times of trouble or crisis, we say all sorts of things that we might not actually believe or feel when we are thinking things through calmly. We could feel forsaken by God in a crisis, but when we are through the crisis, we believe that God has not actually forsaken us. Both can be true—the feeling forsaken and the belief in not having been forsaken.

Probably most people would only choose this meditation during a crisis period, though that crisis could be either a long-term one that requires much time and consideration or an acute crisis that demands an immediate response.

Use this meditation only after some practice with guided imagery and only with plenty of time for reflection afterward. I do not recommend it for a group unless the group members are facing a common crisis, and they agree to work on it through imagery prayer.

MEDITATION: Become quiet and take several slow, deep breaths until you feel relaxed, calm. . . . In your imagination, go to some safe, warm place. Sense yourself surrounded by light; feel the warmth of the light gently surround you. . . .

Now allow a crisis, challenge, or decision to appear before you in your imagination. Observe it from a variety of different angles. If you want to express something to God or to any person, express it in your imagination with as much intensity as you choose. . . . If you want, talk with the Christ; share feelings and ideas. . . . If you need any help or assistance, you can bring that help in, using your imagination.

When you feel that you have expressed your feelings, let yourself complete the dialogue and bid farewell to the people you have invited into your safe place. Remember that you can return to this place in your imagination whenever you choose. Take as long as you need, then when you are ready, affirm amen; open your eyes.

COMMENTS ON DEBRIEFING AND USE: Write out dialogue or draw images that occurred. If you practice this meditation in a group, encourage most to share. In that way, one or two who speak aloud are not left stranded—having shared but not knowing what happened with the others.

The meditation is not directed toward a definite resolution because sometimes a person needs time to fully experience the crisis. Getting in touch with those deep feelings is important along the way toward healing. The answers that emerge may be days, weeks, or months away.

According to the situation, you may want to work toward more resolution during the debriefing period by continuing a dialogue or even by practicing another meditation.

25

A Little Cloud of Hope

[The BIBLICAL NOTE introduces the passage.]

BIBLICAL NOTE: There was conflict in the land regarding who to worship, which religion to adhere to. The prophet Elijah had asked King Ahab to gather on Mount Carmel several hundred prophets from the religion that was competing with the Lord's for the people's devotion. There Elijah had initiated a contest between the many prophets of the other religion and himself, the prophet of the Lord. Each god was asked to start a fire that would consume the bull, which had been laid out as an offering. The god Baal did not come through—no fire started. But Elijah's Lord started a fire that consumed the whole offering.

In the passage for today's meditation, Elijah tells King Ahab to "eat and drink"; that is, break the fast that was being held for the religious ceremony. Elijah refers to the sound of rushing rain, indicating that he has confidence that the horrible drought in the land would soon end. Rain would come. The end of this drought would be final proof that Elijah's Lord ruled. We now see Elijah and his servant at the top of Mount Carmel. Elijah asks his servant to go and check for any evidence of rain. The servant runs to look but reports no evidence—six times. Elijah sends the servant a seventh time, and this time the servant sees a tiny cloud at the horizon. The "tiny cloud" is all Elijah needs as evidence. He sends the servant to tell the king that the rains are coming!

READING: Elijah said to Ahab, "Go up, eat and drink; for there is a sound of rushing rain." So Ahab went up to eat and to drink. Elijah went up to the top of Carmel; there he bowed himself down upon the earth and put his face between his knees. He said to his servant, "Go up now, look toward the sea." He went up and looked, and said, "There is nothing." Then he said, "Go again seven times." At the seventh time he said, "Look, a little cloud no bigger than a person's hand is rising out of the sea." Then

116

he said, "Go say to Ahab, 'Harness your chariot and go down before the rain stops you.'" In a little while the heavens grew black with clouds and wind; there was a heavy rain (1 Kings 18:41-45).

FOR YOUR MEDITATION: In his book *Prayer in Pastoral Counseling,* Ed Wimberly, a pastoral counseling professor, tells of a woman who, in the midst of months of counseling, announced that she was like Elijah. She could not yet see healing in her life, but she knew it was on its way—she had a little cloud of hope. She also saw herself as Elijah's attendant, who had to be obedient to Elijah in order to see the rain come.

MEDITATION: Stand and stretch, if possible. Stretch in several directions. With your arms lifted, take a deep breath, letting the air out as you return your arms to your sides. If you are able, remain standing for this meditation.

　　Get a sense of yourself on a mountaintop. Bow down to sense your connection with the earth and to pray to God. (You may actually bow with your body, as you imagine this.) You can see far in all directions. (You may turn in a circle with your eyes closed to get a feel for the vast expanses in all directions from this mountain.) You have some helpers with you. You are aware of a number of people who are dependent upon you somewhere down that mountain. They await your word. . . . Become aware of what it is they are waiting for. What is it you are looking for on the horizon? . . . Sense the experience of waiting. . . . Looking. . . . Is there hope? . . . When? . . . Ask for help from your attendants, who can check out various facts and features of the landscape for you. . . . Finally one attendant returns to you saying there is a tiny cloud at the horizon. Sense the hope that this brings. However you choose, let the people down the mountain know of your hope. Celebrate! Being aware of your prayerful connection to the earth, this mountain, and to God, bid farewell and amen.

COMMENTS ON DEBRIEFING AND USE: Draw and label the mountain, yourself, and the tiny cloud of hope. (Cotton balls make it three-dimensional.) Hang the image in some well-frequented location to remind yourself that you will not be waiting forever; hope is on the way.

　　It is awkward to present hope in a way that suggests a particular outcome. For example, some may hope for a spouse but never marry. Yet the tiny cloud of hope may signal contentment within a set of relationships that brings joy and fulfillment, even though it is not marriage.

In group sharing, you may find it interesting to discuss ways you "test" God today as Elijah and the prophets of Baal did centuries ago.

26

DETERMINED TO BE HEALED

READING: And a large crowd followed him and pressed in on him. Now there was a woman who had been suffering from hemorrhages for twelve years. She had endured much under many physicians, and had spent all that she had; and she was not better, but rather grew worse. She had heard about Jesus, and came up behind him in the crowd and touched his cloak, for she said, "If I but touch his clothes, I will be made well." Immediately her hemorrhage stopped; and she felt in her body that she was healed of her disease. Immediately aware that power had gone forth from him, Jesus turned about in the crowd and said, "Who touched my clothes?" And his disciples said to him, "You see the crowd pressing in on you; how can you say, 'Who touched me?'" He looked all around to see who had done it. But the woman, knowing what had happened to her, came in fear and trembling, fell down before him, and told him the whole truth. He said to her, "Daughter, your faith has made you well; go in peace, and be healed of your disease" (Mark 5:24-34; see also Matthew 9:20-22; Luke 8:42-48).

BIBLICAL NOTE: The Gospels of Matthew, Mark, and Luke all tell this story. Each time we find it nestled within the story of Jairus's asking Jesus to heal his daughter. After making his request, he and Jesus leave to go to her (Mark 5:21-24; Matthew 9:18-19; Luke 8:40-42). On the way, this woman touches Jesus' clothes and receives healing. Then Jesus continues toward the home of Jairus (Mark 5:35-43; Matthew 9:23-26; Luke 8:49-56).

Jesus makes people whole, healthy, cleansed, and strong—he shows how the reign of God is actually available to people. Those who lived on the margins of society were a priority in Jesus' ministry. It is not surprising that he would attend to an ill woman and a dying child.

The emphasis upon the touch of this woman is crucial for a variety of reasons. First, Jesus' power was so great (and the woman's faith in his power so strong) that by simply touching his clothes, she was healed. Also

Jesus was so attentive to individuals that even while he was pressed against in a crowd he noticed and wanted to meet one particular person who touched him. Finally, the issue of touch was important because this woman was considered permanently unclean due to her hemorrhaging illness. Being labeled "unclean," she was thought to defile anyone whom she touched. Consequently, the crowd could have been very upset at her for touching Jesus. She risked enormous disapproval and danger by reaching out.[15]

Notice the parallels between the healing of this woman and the daughter of Jairus—two females with health problems. One was twelve years old, the other ill for twelve years. One was Jairus's daughter, the other Jesus calls "daughter." Faith was a major element in both healings. While one was brought back from the dead, the other was "as if" dead, for she was "polluted" by her illness, barred from the congregation of supposed holy people.

FOR YOUR MEDITATION: Remember that the healing for which you are determined may be other than physical. For example, you may earnestly desire to be healed of an addiction to a person, situation, or thing. While this story tells of an instantaneous healing, the process toward healing or recovery may take time.

This meditation is presented with you as the woman who touches Jesus. However, you may choose to be a person in the crowd or a disciple, observing someone else who touches Jesus' clothes. You can intentionally place someone whom you know seeks healing in the woman's position as a form of intercessory prayer.

MEDITATION: (If available, play some soothing music in the background.) Take some slow, deep breaths to relax. Let yourself appreciate your body. Notice the many lovely aspects of your body. Touch your body caringly. Take some more breaths and relax.

Visualize yourself in a crowd of people in some setting that feels sacred to you. It may be in a city or a rural area. Sense yourself in the crowd as it anticipates Jesus' arrival. Notice fragrances, sounds, sights, textures. . . .

Now you see the Christ. You are aware of your strong desire for healing. . . . You see the Christ coming nearer. . . . You decide whether to touch the Christ's garments, expecting healing. . . . Make your decision and act as you feel moved. . . . The Christ notices you, out of the crowd.

120

The Christ asks you who you are. Notice your experience. Talk with the Christ as you answer, explaining your situation. . . . The Christ responds to you. . . . The crowd begins to press on, but the Christ looks at you and says, "Daughter [or Son], your faith has made you well; go in peace, and be healed."

Become aware of your experience as the Christ fades out of sight. Notice your body again, appreciating your body, touching it caringly. Consider your relationships, appreciating healthy aspects of your relationships. When you are ready, affirm amen.

COMMENTS ON DEBRIEFING AND USE: Immediately after this meditation, quietly draw or write out what occurred in the interchange between you and the Christ. (Or between the one for whom you are praying and the Christ.) If this meditation was reassuring, place an image or words from it in some location that you will see often to reinforce your sense of healing. If you are practicing this meditation with a group, enlist honest feedback about this visualized encounter.

Because the meditation emphasizes touch, a period of massage of oneself or others would be delightful. People so often need permission to touch one another in healthy ways. (Zach Thomas's book *Healing Touch: The Church's Forgotten Language* is exceptional in reflecting upon this topic.) Touch is so healing! Find someone who knows some massage techniques, or find a book that explains these, and teach each other or yourself how to massage.[16] Or you may celebrate with a "sacrament"—touching yourself or one another with oil as a sign of healing. (Olive oil is fine to use.)

27

THE ANNOUNCEMENT OF BIRTH THROUGH YOU

READING: And [the angel Gabriel] came to her and said, "Greetings, favored one! The Lord is with you." But she was much perplexed by his words and pondered what sort of greeting this might be. The angel said to her, "Do not be afraid, Mary, for you have found favor with God. And now, you will conceive in your womb and bear a son, and you will name him Jesus" (Luke 1:28-31).

BIBLICAL NOTE: In the first two chapters of the Gospel of Luke, we read stories of annunciation, special births, circumcisions, namings, and presentations that alternate between John the Baptist and Jesus. In both stories, the angel Gabriel announces the birth. As with other saving figures of the Hebrew Scriptures, after the announcement of birth, the immediate reaction is fear. Then a message of God's intent is delivered. The one to whom birth is promised objects at first but then is given a sign for comfort and hope.

FOR YOUR MEDITATION: Whether you are male or female, you can experience birth in many ways: the birth of a project in your life; the birth of a gift to offer your family, your community, the world; the birth of an idea; the birth of a child. In this meditation allow yourself to be open to the many meanings of birth. I am using *wise person* rather than an *angel* as the messenger in this meditation. The wise person for you may be a friend or someone whom you respect. Or it may be a symbol or an unknown voice. You do not need to know now what it will be; simply enter into meditation and let it appear.

MEDITATION: Sit quietly and relax, taking a few deep breaths. . . . Allow yourself to let go of thoughts or tensions. . . . Simply let go. . . . Now imagine a wise person appearing before you. This wise person speaks to you saying, "Do not be afraid, for God has been gracious to you; you are about to give birth. . . ." Hear the words, *You are about to give birth* again. Notice your experience. . . . Feel free to communicate with the symbol of wisdom. . . . You may want to understand more completely what this birth is. . . . If so, allow yourself to focus on this birth; explore it as long as you need to. . . . If you are not clear about what is being announced, just let yourself sense the feeling of expectancy. . . . When you are ready, say good-bye to the wise person. Reflect on your feelings about the expected birth. . . . Give thanks for the potential within you, and open your eyes.

COMMENTS ON DEBRIEFING AND USE: This meditation requires a period of silence afterward simply to let the message soak in. Because this meditation may be abstract, remember the three levels of meanings for images, discussed in chapter 1. You may draw the wise person or the expected birth. Write down what has been announced, so it will be clearer to you.

You could fill out an "Announcement of Birth," or a "Birth Certificate." If you place this announcement on a wall, it may continue to evoke the sense of birth through you. Look at the "Announcement of Birth" a month later to see what has taken place; look again ten months later!

28

TEMPTATIONS

READING: Then Jesus was led up by the Spirit into the wilderness to be tempted by the devil. He fasted forty days and forty nights, and afterwards he was famished. The tempter came and said to him, "If you are the Son of God, command these stones to become loaves of bread." But he answered, "It is written,

'One does not live by bread alone,
but by every word that comes
from the mouth of God.'"

Then the devil took him to the holy city and placed him on the pinnacle of the temple, saying to him, "If you are the Son of God, throw yourself down; for it is written,

'He will command his angels
concerning you,'
and 'On their hands they will
bear you up,
so that you will not dash your
foot against a stone.'"

Jesus said to him, "Again it is written, 'Do not put the Lord your God to the test.'"

Again, the devil took him to a very high mountain and showed him all the kingdoms of the world and their splendor; and he said to him, "All these I will give you, if you will fall down and worship me." Jesus said to him, "Away with you, Satan! for it is written,

'Worship the Lord your God,
and serve only him.'"

Then the devil left him, and suddenly angels came and waited on him (Matthew 4:1-11; see also Mark 1:12-13; Luke 4:1-13).

BIBLICAL NOTE: The three versions of the wilderness temptations differ greatly and are worth comparing. In Matthew the wilderness temptations occur just before Jesus begins his public ministry, shortly after his baptism. They help to clarify Jesus' purpose in relation to the hopes of Israel.

In both Matthew and Luke, we find that Jesus is famished, and the tempter takes advantage of his hunger. Perhaps he could tempt Jesus to become a "miracle-worker," like one of the so-called "divine men" of ancient days.[17] Jesus might turn a stone into bread. But Jesus refuses to use his power in this way, explaining that his power is his trust in God's will.

The second temptation offers Jesus the opportunity to be a super hero—flinging himself off a high mountain, leaping sensationally without being hurt. It is the power to transcend natural laws. Jesus modestly refuses, indicating that he is not going to "test" God. He willingly cooperates with gravity as a human.

Political power, the rule over all the kingdoms, was the third temptation. Jesus resisted again as he sought to let God guide him, in due time—no instant promises.

FOR YOUR MEDITATION: We are often tempted to pray for specific needs, using God to provide for us just what we want. We are tempted to ask for some type of certainty in our life, some guaranteed security. Some of us are tempted to seek power over other people in relationships rather than recognizing our own integrity and that of others. Experience this meditation as a way to become more aware of how you deal with these temptations. If you are content, recognize this. If you are dissatisfied, then you may choose to change.

MEDITATION: Sit quietly and take a few deep breaths. . . . Now imagine a large blank sheet of paper in front of you and see the words: *Temptation Number One.* . . . See written on that paper *Wanting above all else to satisfy immediate needs.* . . . Notice whatever occurs for you, times you have wanted to satisfy your needs immediately. . . . Simply acknowledge what appears and let it be. . . . [You might want to jot this down on paper with your eyes open, then close them again and continue.] Another large clean sheet of paper appears with the words: *Temptation Number Two.* You see the phrase *Wanting certainty or proof of security.* . . . Think of ways you have been tempted to seek certainty or proof of security. Reflect on the feelings that emerge for you. . . . [Jot down notes.] Now on a third large sheet of paper you see the words: *Temptation Number Three.* Wait a moment, then notice the phrase *Wanting power or control over others.*

. . . Think about that phrase in relation to your life, times you have been tempted to have power or control over others rather than relating as equals. . . . [Jot down notes.] Recall what has occurred for you as you have considered these three temptations. . . . Call upon the Christ or any other person or symbol that you choose. Dialogue with that person or image. . . . Allow some guidance or resolution to emerge. . . . As you discuss your experience, you might imagine going out into the sunlight to find greater warmth and light. . . . Take whatever time you need. . . . Wait for guidance and new understanding. . . . Experience being accepted by God. . . . When you feel ready, open your eyes.

COMMENTS ON DEBRIEFING AND USE: This exercise involves both a confrontation and a sense of achievement. I believe that we grow in this way. Share with a friend or a group what occurred for you, so that you can discuss the temptations and your relationship to God. You could draw the three sheets of paper with the accompanying insights. Notice any gender or age biases in the kinds of temptations.

29

No Longer Jew or Greek, Slave or Free, Male and Female

READING: For in Christ Jesus you are all children of God through faith. As many of you as were baptized into Christ have clothed yourselves with Christ. There is no longer Jew or Greek, there is no longer slave or free, there is no longer male and female; for all of you are one in Christ Jesus. And if you belong to Christ, then you are Abraham's offspring, heirs according to the promise (Galatians 3:26-29; see also 1 Corinthians 12:12-13; Colossians 3:9-11).

BIBLICAL NOTE: These passages in Galatians, First Corinthians, and Colossians present what probably was an early Christian confession made by those who became Christians before Paul was influential. The three texts are not identical, but that is typical for traditions that originate and spread orally.[18] Paul thought of baptism as initiation into a new community in which distinctions among races, social classes, and gender no longer applied.

FOR YOUR MEDITATION: This is a valuable passage upon which to meditate with a group of diverse persons. You may use it in settings in which there is conflict over what constitutes "equality." It is valuable also with those who are celebrating a "new equality." Or those who are painfully aware of inequality may use the meditation.

MEDITATION: Stretch your body and relax. Take some slow, deep breaths. Find a comfortable position. . . . Notice your body: its textures, shape, size, how it feels to be you. . . . Now imagine clear, cleansing water being poured over your head, flowing onto your whole body. Sense the temperature, the sensations, the movement of the water as it touches your body. . . . Experience yourself as baptized, a good creation, renewed in Christ, clothed in Christ. . . .

In your imagination see others who are being baptized—those who are of different nationalities . . . those of various ethnic backgrounds, . . . people thought of as slaves and those perceived to be free . . . males and females. . . . Witness this cleansing, clear water being poured over all these people. . . . Experience all as baptized, good creations, renewed in Christ, clothed in Christ. . . .

Now allow yourself to see all these who are baptized interacting with one another. Imagine the new humanity. . . . Perhaps you see people you recognize. Feel free to interact. . . . Sense yourself to be heirs in common with all these people. Let yourself know that, experience it.

The Christ is present even now. Be aware of your physical environment, whether you are alone or with others, and slowly open your eyes, affirming your baptism.

COMMENTS ON DEBRIEFING AND USE: Create murals with overlapping images of the baptized or make masks. This meditation could generate much discussion since people have different experiences of their own baptism and their understanding of others' baptisms.

30

GETTING A SENSE OF YOUR GROWTH

READING: [Jesus] also said, "The kingdom of God is as if someone would scatter seed on the ground, and would sleep and rise night and day, and the seed would sprout and grow, he does not know how. The earth produces of itself, first the stalk, then the head, then the full grain in the head. But when the grain is ripe, at once he goes in with his sickle, because the harvest has come" (Mark 4:26-29).

BIBLICAL NOTE: This is one of three different parables about seeds. This one shows the mystery of growth, which is beyond our control. The Greek word *basileia*, which is translated "kingdom" has a dynamic sense to it, captured better by our current English word *reign*. The reign of God is dynamic, growing mysteriously, just as seeds transform into harvest—in time but virtually inevitably.

FOR YOUR MEDITATION: You could think of a particular "seed" in your life (profession, relationship, hobby, discipline, or child), upon which to focus in this meditation. Or you could let this meditation reflect your life in general. Alternately, you could think of the whole reign of God.

This meditation would be highly appropriate for an Earth Day celebration! It could yield both an appreciation of the earth and its harvest as well as a confession about our attempts to bring in a vision of the future that is unlike the one of which Jesus spoke.

MEDITATION: Take a few deep breaths, sitting in an upright, straight position, if possible. Imagine yourself to be at the seaside. . . . Feel the sand below your feet, warm and supportive. . . . Feel the warmth of the sun bathing your body with its rays. . . . Look around to see what is there. . . . Notice any rocks, greenery, animals, or people. . . . Now as you walk along the sand, notice a group of people further down the beach. . . . Gradually walk up to them and observe that one seems to be teaching the others—that one is the Christ. As you mingle with the crowd, you find that the Christ is handing a seed to everyone. The Christ says to you that the seed represents your life or some aspect of your life, sustained and nurtured by God. . . . You receive your seed. . . . Walk away to wherever you want to go to plant your seed. . . . Plant it. Let it grow and watch it unfold and mature. . . . What is happening to it? What stage is it in? . . . You may· want to communicate with your growing seed; it may have a message for you. Be open to whatever happens. . . . When you feel ready, move back to the warm, sandy beach, remembering your seed. Become aware of the many seeds growing around the earth. Affirm amen.

COMMENTS ON DEBRIEFING AND USE: This meditation is very help-ful in developing self-awareness. Definitely you will change. It is impor-tant not to become attached to this symbol whether you are excited by it, confronted, or disappointed. You might stay alert to magazine pictures or photos that fit your image or draw one yourself. If a group joins in this, you could make a mural of "Our Growth."

31

PURITY LAWS OR INNER MOTIVATION?

READING: While [Jesus] was speaking, a Pharisee invited him to dine with him; and he went in and took his place at the table. The Pharisee was amazed to see that he did not first wash before dinner. Then the Lord said to him, "Now you Pharisees clean the outside of the cup and of the dish, but inside you are full of greed and wickedness. You fools! Did not the one who made the outside make the inside also? So give for alms those things that are within; and see, everything will be clean for you. But woe to you Pharisees! For you tithe mint and rue and herbs of all kinds, and neglect justice and the love of God; it is these you ought to have practiced, without neglecting the others" (Luke 11:37-42; also see Matthew 23:25-26; Mark 7:3-4).

BIBLICAL NOTE: The Pharisees were a group that went through distinct phases, from the second century B.C.E. to the end of the second century C.E. They started out primarily as a political party within the Jewish royal court; then under the leadership of Hillel, they withdrew from the political arena and became an association of men who committed themselves to the precise observance of the Torah, or Law. After the First Jewish War (66–70 C.E..), they again were a political power who gradually became the supreme Jewish authorities. At the time of Jesus, they were primarily involved in maintaining spiritual purity, not by separating themselves from other Jews or Gentiles but by being quite precise about their observance, household by household. They set themselves apart from the ordinary Jews, thus creating a barrier between themselves and other Jews. But this meticulous piety also provided them with a particular identity—clean. Outsiders were characterized as "habitually unclean."

Jesus rejected the Pharisees' concern for the cleanliness of hands. The Gospel of Luke presents him as being far more concerned with the purity of intent than with maintaining strict Jewish purity laws about what, how, and with whom one eats. In Luke's Gospel, Jesus does not say that Christians should not practice the purity laws of the Jews (in fact, some of the early Christians were Pharisees). Jesus argues that one should be *as* concerned about claims for justice, love, and intent to do good as the "externals" of religion.

The Gospel of Mark presents Jesus even more radically as one who has dismissed physical purity as a matter of religious concern. For example, Mark indicates that Jesus declared all foods clean (Mark 7:18-19). Matthew's Gospel also depicts Jesus as declaring a new purity—the purity of the heart.

FOR YOUR MEDITATION: This meditation fits naturally with many people's reflections at bedtime, as an evening review of the day. In a worship setting, a congregation could practice it for the prayer of confession. It is especially relevant to worship themes or discussions that pertain to the body and to possessions, for Jewish "purity" and "property" laws regulated these areas. It is important to understand Jesus as a Jew, engaging in discussions with other Jews.

MEDITATION: Become quiet and take a few slow, deep breaths. . . . Feel that breath moving through your entire body as you let go of tensions and feel strength within you. . . . Now slowly review the day (or week or month), thinking of things you have done, things about which you feel good. . . . You may start in the morning and move through the day, affirming yourself for the actions, activities, external deeds and accomplishments that fit into your concept of *good*. . . . Now think back through the day, reflecting upon how you might have been kinder or more just; consider what you might have done. . . . Imagine yourself choosing these kinder, wiser, or more just ways. . . . Imagine clear water pouring over your body, cleansing you on the outside.

Turn your attention within. . . . Become aware how you felt and what you thought of your experiences this day. Remember the thoughts and feelings that were constructive to life. . . . Now recall those thoughts and feelings that were not constructive to life, either your life or the lives of others. . . . Imagine yourself thinking or feeling in more life-enhancing ways. . . . Take time to imagine this, to imagine engaging with other people with this purity of intent. Now imagine clear water pouring through the inside of your being—cleansing you inside. Get a sense of yourself being clean within.

Notice any feelings or thoughts that remain, thoughts that leave you feeling not quite cleansed. . . . When you have done this, sit quietly for a few minutes and let your mind be as still as possible. If any thoughts emerge, acknowledge them. Simply sit quietly. . . . When you feel finished, open your eyes.

COMMENTS ON DEBRIEFING AND USE: People are very different. Some of us attend to our every word, thought, and action, questioning its goodness—looking for improvement. Others of us scarcely look at our behavior or thoughts at all; a little self-reflection would do us good. Consider these differences as you reflect upon this meditation.

Looking back over the day, week, or month helps us gain a fresh perspective. I hope this meditation affirms the good, while acknowledging what needs improvement or cleansing. Feeling miserable about oneself as "unclean" is unproductive. Just as we cannot will forgiveness, so moving toward purity of intent is not entirely an act of will. We can intend to have pure intent, but it's a gradual process in which God's grace is an important factor.

Draw yourself as a vessel, using words or symbols that represent what was affirmed and cleansed away—on the outside and the inside. This whole practice can be done with a joyful, as well as challenging, spirit.

32

Holy, Humble, Indefatigable, and Healed

READING: From there [Jesus] set out and went away to the region of Tyre. He entered a house and did not want anyone to know he was there. Yet he could not escape notice, but a woman whose little daughter had an unclean spirit immediately heard about him, and she came and bowed down at his feet. Now the woman was a Gentile, of Syrophoenician origin. She begged him to cast the demon out of her daughter. He said to her, "Let the children be fed first, for it is not fair to take the children's food and throw it to the dogs." But she answered him, "Sir, even the dogs under the table eat the children's crumbs." Then he said to her, "For saying that, you may go—the demon has left your daughter." So she went home, found the child lying on the bed, and the demon gone (Mark 7:24-30; see also Matthew 15:21-28).

BIBLICAL NOTE: This woman, a Phoenician from Syria, is the only person in the entire Gospel of Mark to win an argument with Jesus. We know little about the woman (name, marital status, economic level) except that she has a demon-possessed daughter and is identified as a Gentile. Jairus also had bowed at Jesus' feet, begging Jesus to heal his daughter, but Jairus was a Jewish male of high status. To Jairus, Jesus responded willingly and quickly. Even though Jesus had already healed a foreigner and even though this woman behaves with honorable deference to him in a private setting, Jesus insults her by likening her to a dog![19]

New Testament professor Thomas Boomershine in his book *Story Journey* suggests that the woman would make such a request either out of arrogance or humility. He concludes that it is humility, because she sets aside all assumptions of her superiority by asking a Jew to heal, by making herself vulnerable, and by crossing the boundary to an "enemy."

Jesus is presented here as thinking that he is called to minister only to Jews. He would not waste his "food" on "dogs," those who were not Israelites. This woman doesn't argue with the comparison to dogs; she reframes it, transforming the dog into a house pet, thus appealing for a new relationship to Jesus. At least she can have the scraps that fall from the table of the (Jewish) children!

This woman was holy, pious with respect to Jesus, and filled with faith. She was humble, not defending herself, her nationality, or her race—even when insulted. She was indefatigable—her daughter *would* receive Jesus' blessing. As a result, her daughter was healed.

FOR YOUR MEDITATION: In practicing this meditation, many people will identify with this woman to some degree. Some may identify with Jesus as one from whom others ask for gifts. A third alternative is to observe the two interacting with each other. The requested healing need not be physical. The request may be for something you greatly desire but feel is out of reach, foreign to you , or uncustomary to ask for.

Consider using this meditation at an ecumenical setting with Jews and Christians; it has many levels of religious boundary-crossings.

MEDITATION: Stretch, take a little walk, or move around to get your body alert and relaxed. Take a few deep breaths and sit in silence for a little while. . . . Imagine being at a coastal town, walking along a road. . . . You realize that you are coming to a house in which the Christ rests. . . . Become aware of a request you would like to make of him. . . . Now consider whether you want to go to the Christ to make this request. . . . Notice whether you feel in some way less worthy than others or underappreciated. Get in touch with your own inner strength and sense of value. . . . If you choose to, knock on the door and make yourself known. You introduce yourself and, paying due respect, make your request. . . . The Christ responds in a shocking way, comparing you to others or undervaluing you. Stand up for yourself! Be clear regarding your need and purpose. Continue to interact until you arrive at satisfaction. You realize that you are now ready to go, and you bid farewell. . . . Walk on down the road in the coastal town in your imagination, considering the satisfactory outcome until you feel ready to open your eyes and say amen.

COMMENTS ON DEBRIEFING AND USE: No one can guarantee that your request will be granted. However, to make the request, to feel your worth, and to be valued is significant! Write out your feelings.

33

FEEDING THE HUNGRY

READING: After this Jesus went to the other side of the Sea of Galilee, also called the Sea of Tiberias. A large crowd kept following him, because they saw the signs that he was doing for the sick. Jesus went up the mountain and sat down there with his disciples. Now the Passover, the festival of the Jews, was near. When he looked up and saw a large crowd coming toward him, Jesus said to Philip, "Where are we to buy bread for these people to eat?" He said this to test him, for he himself knew what he was going to do. Philip answered him, "Six months' wages would not buy enough bread for each of them to get a little." One of his disciples, Andrew, Simon Peter's brother, said to him, "There is a boy here who has five barley loaves and two fish. But what are they among so many people?" Jesus said, "Make the people sit down." Now there was a great deal of grass in the place; so they sat down, about five thousand in all. Then Jesus took the loaves, and when he had given thanks, he distributed them to those who were seated; so also the fish, as much as they wanted. When they were satisfied, he told his disciples, "Gather up the fragments left over, so that nothing may be lost." So they gathered them up, and from the fragments of the five barley loaves, left by those who had eaten, they filled twelve baskets. When the people saw the sign that he had done, they began to say, "This is indeed the prophet who is to come into the world" (John 6:1-14; see also Matthew 14:13-21; Mark 6:30-44; Luke 9:10-17).

BIBLICAL NOTE: One of the many meals of Jesus' ministry, this is the only miracle recorded in all four Gospels. Jesus takes charge, acting with compassion for the crowd that has followed him persistently.

Barley bread was a common food of the poor people. Fish was a delicacy, eaten as a relish with the bread. Early Christian art used bread and fish as symbols of the Eucharist.

FOR YOUR MEDITATION: You might think of hunger in the literal sense, expressing concern for local, national, or world hunger. Or you might consider hunger in the metaphorical sense, focusing upon spiritual or intellectual hunger, or hunger for meaning.

MEDITATION: Take three deep breaths. . . . Get a sense of yourself walking along a beach. . . . Become aware of how hard or soft the sand is below your feet. Notice whether there are any other people—or any other forms of life. . . . Sense the fragrance of this beach. . . . Observe the colors of the water and sand. . . . It is a warm and sunny day. Feel that warmth moving through your body. . . . Now become aware that you are holding a picnic basket. As you walk along the beach, you notice a figure at the top of a small hill. . . . You realize as you get closer that the figure is the Christ. . . . You climb up this small hill to greet the Christ. Greet each other and communicate in whatever way is right for you. . . . As you sit or stand, talking with each other, the Christ asks you what you have in your picnic basket. . . . You open it and present what is there. As you talk about the food, you mention that there are people who are hungry. You ask how these people are to be fed. Wait for some answer. . . . Allow some guidance to occur. . . . See what your responsibility is. . . . If you want to, go ahead and eat the bread or picnic lunch, taking the action that is asked of you. . . . Now it is time to say good-bye. . . . Become aware how you feel as you bid farewell to the Christ. . . . Continue to walk down to the beach. Reflect upon this event. . . . When you are ready, open your eyes.

COMMENTS ON DEBRIEFING AND USE: This meditation is appropriate for practice by one (alone—perhaps before eating), a family, a church dinner, or a large gathering. It may accompany a love feast or the Eucharist. It would be appropriate in conjunction with sharing by the hungry or learning information about the hungry in your community. Persons will hold many views about what actually happened in the biblical passage. Focus upon the images that emerged, sharing the guidance each received.

Each person could say aloud what gifts she or he brings to the community; that is, what "loaves and fishes" (talents, service, prayers, money) she or he has to offer to the whole community. If this is done, the meditation would be applicable for an event that names officers, expresses appreciation of volunteers, or accepts new members.

34

THE TENDER LOVE OF
A MOTHER HEN

READING: "Jerusalem, Jerusalem, the city that kills the prophets and stones those who are sent to it! How often have I desired to gather your children together as a hen gathers her brood under her wings, and you were not willing! See, your house is left to you, desolate. For I tell you, you will not see me again until you say, 'Blessed is the one who comes in the name of the Lord'" (Matthew 23:37-39; see also Luke 13:34-35).

BIBLICAL NOTE: Jesus speaks out of tender love for Jerusalem, mourning Jerusalem's children. In so doing, he identifies himself with female roles, not only by speaking of himself metaphorically as a mother hen but also by taking on the role of a public mourner. The mourner for the community traditionally was a woman.[20]

FOR YOUR MEDITATION: You could draw a picture of a mother hen, gathering her brood, protecting them under her wings, before you practice this meditation. Then begin your meditation as you look at the mother hen picture.

If you practice this meditation in a group, discuss how birds protect their young. Consider other metaphors that produce a sense of tender caring.

This is an excellent meditation for a time of crisis. It can offer comfort. It is also useful when you are providing care for others—as a way of experiencing yourself being cared for simultaneously.

MEDITATION: Stretch, relax, and take some slow, deep breaths. Visualize yourself in some familiar nature area: a meadow, a farmland, a sandy beach, or a warm spot on a mountain. . . . Let yourself observe this spot in nature. Hear any sounds, smell fragrances, feel the textures. . . . Notice whether you are alone or with others. . . . Now name some concern you have or some need you have. This may be for yourself or others. Imagine being gathered in, pulled gently under a wing. You realize a Mother Hen has pulled you toward her, protecting you. Let yourself be gathered in, cared for. Experience safety, warmth, and care. Stay there as long as you desire, feeling her care. . . . You may either stay there and affirm amen or move from under the wing, back to the familiar nature area, continuing to feel the tender care.

COMMENTS ON DEBRIEFING AND USE: Draw, sculpt, sew, dance, or sing your experience under the wing of the mother hen. If practiced in a group, you could form pairs. Each pair can choose one art form through which to share their experience with the rest of the group.

35

FINDING WHAT WAS LOST

READING: "Or what woman having ten silver coins, if she loses one of them, does not light a lamp, sweep the house, and search carefully until she finds it? When she has found it, she calls together her friends and neighbors, saying, 'Rejoice with me, for I have found the coin that I had lost.' Just so, I tell you, there is joy in the presence of the angels of God over one sinner who repents" (Luke 15:8-10).

BIBLICAL NOTE: The Gospel of Luke situates this parable between the parable of the lost sheep and the parable of the lost son. Through this parable, Jesus expresses his conviction that God cares for all humanity—even, or especially, those who seem (to themselves or to others) lost. Jesus compares God first to a shepherd, then to a woman house sweeper, and finally to the father of two sons.

Notice the similar sequence: The woman has, loses, sweeps and seeks until she finds, then rejoices. The shepherd has, loses, leaves until he finds, then rejoices. This sequence is followed by an explanation that there is joy in heaven over one repentant sinner.

Palestinian homes had few windows; probably the woman needed a lamp to search for the coins. Ten coins could have been a life savings for a poor woman in Palestine at that time.

FOR YOUR MEDITATION: The valuables in this meditation may be possessions, ideas or beliefs, relationships, activities, or even memories. You actually may be able to find one of these lost items; however, some of these items can be recovered only in a changed state. Do not be concerned that you must find what is lost; simply remain aware of what is occurring in your imagery.

MEDITATION: Take three or more slow, deep breaths. Allow yourself to feel calm, centered, and relaxed. . . . Now experience yourself within a home. Look around to notice what kind of home it is: how it is decorated; where the windows are; what furniture is present; what colors, fragrances, and sounds are in this home. . . . Walk over to where you keep your valuables and look at them. . . . You realize you have lost something that is worth a great deal to you. . . . Become aware of your feelings as you discover the loss. . . . Stand there, experiencing this loss. . . . Now you begin to search for this. If you would like to turn on a light, get a lamp, or use a flashlight, do that. . . . Now search all over, wherever you need to look. . . . How do you feel as you search? . . . Take time. . . . You find it! Or you find it in some form. It may have changed. . . . Stay aware of your experience. . . . Go back to where the rest of your valuables are. . . . Note how you feel now that you have found what you had lost. . . . If it has changed, sense your feelings about that change. . . . If you want to, call a friend or neighbor, explain what has happened, and share your thoughts and feelings. If appropriate, rejoice!

Think back over the experience of losing, then finding something. Sit in silence until you are ready, then open your eyes.

COMMENTS ON DEBRIEFING AND USE: Spend some time naming, listing, expressing how it was to find something precious to you that was lost. Then discuss or write about how this might be similar to how God feels when we are "found" by God. Take an empathetic leap to imagine God's perspective, given your meditation practice.

Draw the house, valuables, or your expression when you discovered the loss and when you found it. Draw fanciful images of God as you imagine God to "feel" when God discovers a loss and again finds that which was lost.

Look again at the three levels of meaning explained in chapter 1.

36

THE POOR'S RIGHTS FOR JUSTICE

READING: Then Jesus told them a parable about their need to pray always and not to lose heart. He said, "In a certain city there was a judge who neither feared God nor had respect for people. In that city there was a widow who kept coming to him and saying, 'Grant me justice against my opponent.' For a while he refused; but later he said to himself, 'Though I have no fear of God and no respect for anyone, yet because this widow keeps bothering me, I will grant her justice, so that she may not wear me out by continually coming.'" And the Lord said, "Listen to what the unjust judge says. And will not God grant justice to his chosen ones who cry to him day and night? Will he delay long in helping them? I tell you, he will quickly grant justice to them. And yet, when the Son of Man comes, will he find faith on earth?" (Luke 18:1-8).

BIBLICAL NOTE: Those who aren't poor (and sometimes the poor themselves) often perceive poverty as personal failure. However, in Israel at the time of Jesus, poverty was also considered injustice. Jesus addressed this injustice again and again as he proclaimed the *basileia*, the reign of God, to the poor. He was not simply saying the poor will receive some future reward, but that the poor had rights within God's justice now.

Here Jesus suggests that if the uncaring judge finally grants justice to the persistent widow, then God, who does care, would certainly grant justice to those who keep asking.

FOR YOUR MEDITATION: Many people consider themselves "for" justice, siding with those who are poor or oppressed. Yet actually speaking up for others or oneself is often a step that is taken reluctantly, if at all. I wrestle with this issue in my book *When You Need to Take a Stand*, especially in the chapters: "When and How to Speak," "Empowering Others to Speak," and "When You Don't Think You Have Enough Power."

This meditation would be an excellent opening for an event regarding a social or political issue. People can be encouraged to speak through letter writing, attending meetings, speaking to appropriate groups and committees, or petitioning or picketing. An individual can practice this meditation in the midst of taking stands, to gain clarity and to sustain motivation.

This passage may raise the questions: Isn't it enough to pray one time for a specific request? Doesn't God respond the first time? Your theological view determines the answer for you. I suggest that the answer is, "Yes, *and* persistence in asking may clarify issues for *ourselves*, paving the way for answers."

MEDITATION: Take a few deep breaths. Feel yourself sustained by your chair or the floor. Let your weight be carried by that on which you sit, as you let your body be rooted, grounded. . . . In your mind's eye get a sense of yourself in a sacred place. It may be a church, synagogue, or a place of nature. Notice the surroundings, the colors, the sounds. See the details of this sacred place. . . .

Now a person who represents justice arrives. . . . You reflect upon a request for justice that you seek to make for yourself or for others. Decide whether and how you will ask. . . . If you are ready, go up to the person who represents justice, make your request, then return to your place. . . . Do this again, making your request a second time. . . . Let the one who represents justice respond to you—interact. . . . Ask again a number of times, each time waiting for a response. . . . Continue to ask until you receive some guidance about your request or clarity that you are finished asking.

When you sense that you are finished, again experience yourself being in this sacred place. Notice the surroundings, colors, and sounds. Sit in silence. Recall your experience with asking and the answers you received. When you are ready, affirm amen.

COMMENTS ON DEBRIEFING AND USE: While reflection upon action or potential action is useful, actually *taking* action on behalf of the poor or oppressed would be an appropriate completion to this meditation.

Personal reflection upon (or group discussion about) patience—what to do in the "meantime" is valuable here. Between the asking, the asking again, and the granting of the request, what does one do?—Figure out how to ask once more? Take yet another action?

37

LETTING GO OF ANXIETY—
ACCEPTING GOD'S PROVISIONS

READING: [Jesus] said to his disciples, "That's why I tell you: don't fret about life—what you're going to eat—or about your body—what you're going to wear. Remember, there is more to living than food and clothing. Think about the crows: they don't plant or harvest, they don't have storerooms or barns. Yet God feeds them. You're worth a lot more than the birds! Can any of you add an hour to life by fretting about it? So if you can't do a little thing like that, why worry about the rest? Think about how the lilies grow: they don't slave and they never spin. Yet let me tell you, even Solomon at the height of his glory was never decked out like one of them. If God dresses up the grass in the field, which is here today and tomorrow is tossed into an oven, it is surely more likely (that God cares for) you, you who don't take anything for granted! And don't be constantly on the lookout for what you're going to eat and what you're going to drink. Don't give it a thought. These are all things the world's pagans seek, and your Father is aware that you need them. Instead, you are to seek (God's) domain, and these things will come to you as a bonus (Luke 12:22-31, *The Complete Gospels*; see also Matthew 6:25-34).

BIBLICAL NOTE: The main thrust of this passage is that worry need not distract us. God has given us life. Since life is such a large, inclusive gift, we can certainly expect that God will also give us enough food and clothing. For most of us, worries *are* unnecessary; yet we live with the discomforting fact that many people in today's world are starving. A tension exists between faith and social facts.

"Lilies" could refer to any number of wild flowers. The teaching and metaphors used here have many roots in Jewish writings. Make the images relevant to your particular context.

FOR YOUR MEDITATION: Starvation, malnutrition, and poverty exist in many forms. Yet there's also abundant life and sustenance. We can focus upon the need for human love to encourage equitable distribution and intelligence to maintain wise policies. For this meditation you could intentionally choose not to worry—even for others—focusing *entirely* upon the abundant gift of life.

MEDITATION: Take three deep breaths and relax as you exhale, letting go of tensions and anxieties. . . . When you are still, visualize a flower before you. Observe this flower, noticing the colors, fragrance, texture . . . beauty. . . . Notice this flower in as much detail as you can. . . . Now become aware of the life flowing through this flower. Think of the nutrients, the water in the soil that nourish the flower. . . . Sense the harmony between this flower, its environment, and the larger environment. . . .

Now become aware of yourself. Pay attention to your body. Notice any part that seems tense. . . . Reflect on your emotions and any concerns you may be experiencing. . . . Pay attention to your thoughts. . . . Let go of these tensions, concerns, and thoughts as you experience your rootedness in life. . . . Sense the flowing of God's life through you. . . . Compare yourself to this flower, as you are being provided for. . . . Let worry evaporate as you simply live, cared for as you express yourself naturally.

As you experience God's providing for the flower and for you, extend your consciousness to include persons throughout the world. Think of many people and living things throughout the world. . . . Note any resistance or barriers to every living being's adequate provision . . . . Now take a large leap in your mind to let go of any thought about these needs or worries for provision. Imagine God's domain on earth. . . . Imagine creative ways of interacting, of doing research, of using renewable resources. Imagine justice. . . . Think big. . . . Imagine the enjoyment of peoples and environments. See God's reign with peace and justice. Now see again the flower, its beauty. Affirm with gratitude amen.

COMMENTS ON DEBRIEFING AND USE: A family may use this meditation when uncertain about provision for basic needs. By staying alert to the simple necessities of the flower, we realize that the purpose is not that God gives us any particular thing but that we are occupied with bigger issues. Consider practicing this meditation at a church function that emphasizes world concerns, world hunger, the environment, or justice in the community.

38

CHANGING OUR WAYS; CHANGING GOD'S MIND?

READING: The word of the Lord came to Jonah a second time, saying, "Get up, go to Nineveh, that great city, and proclaim to it the message that I tell you." So Jonah set out and went to Nineveh, according to the word of the Lord. Now Nineveh was an exceedingly large city, a three days' walk across. Jonah began to go into the city, going a day's walk. And he cried out, "Forty days more, and Nineveh shall be overthrown!" And the people of Nineveh believed God; they proclaimed a fast, and everyone, great and small, put on sackcloth.

When the news reached the king of Nineveh, he rose from his throne, removed his robe, covered himself with sackcloth, and sat in ashes. Then he had a proclamation made in Nineveh: "By the decree of the king and his nobles: No human being or animal, no herd or flock, shall taste anything. They shall not feed, nor shall they drink water. Human beings and animals shall be covered with sackcloth, and they shall cry mightily to God. All shall turn from their evil ways and from the violence that is in their hands. Who knows? God may relent and change his mind; he may turn from his fierce anger, so that we do not perish."

When God saw what they did, how they turned from their evil ways, God changed his mind about the calamity that he had said he would bring upon them; and he did not do it (Jonah 3:1-10).

BIBLICAL NOTE: Read the whole book of Jonah; it is only four chapters, the third of which is cited here. Jonah is a prophet of the eighth century B.C.E. about whom there is a brief reference in 2 Kings 14:25. The book of Jonah is satirical, yet about serious matters. It is very funny, a "comedy of horrors";[21] at the same time soberingly sad and joyous.

Earlier God had asked Jonah to pronounce judgment upon Nineveh, but Jonah fled. His attempted escape began with boarding a ship that was traveling to Tarshish, but Jonah ended up in the stomach of a fish. Now God asks Jonah again. Notice that Jonah does not tell the city folk to repent; he simply announces God's intentions as he walks through Nineveh.

To the reader's (and perhaps God's) amazement, the entire population repents. At the king's request, each person (and animal) puts on a sackcloth. Then they "turn from their evil ways" and from "violence." Like the persistent widow (Meditation 36), they cry out again and again to God for help.

Then God changes God's mind! God will not cause the calamity.

This isn't the end of the story. Jonah is upset with God because Jonah didn't think the Ninevites deserved God's grace. That's why Jonah fled to begin with: He knew that God was "merciful, slow to anger, and abounding in steadfast love, and ready to relent from punishing" (Jonah 4:2). He didn't want to see the Ninevites forgiven. In fact, he'd rather die. Before the story's end God cleverly teaches Jonah the compassion that God feels for the people.

FOR YOUR MEDITATION: World events are always in such a state of flux that inevitably some city or situation is in need of repentance. This passage remains relevant.

On a smaller, individual scale, almost everyone has some person about whom they feel as Jonah does about Nineveh. "Why should she get off scot-free?"

I love two things about this passage. First, we see that people, a large number of people, *can change*! In fact, they can give up their evil ways and their violence! What more hopeful image for us than to envision ourselves to be like the Ninevites! It may be worth making pronouncements, talking about environmental crises, insisting upon change to renewable resources, working for arms reduction and an end to violence. People can change. Second, this passage shows God *changing God's mind*! A lot of people think of God as unchangeable, which so often means they don't really believe God is responsive to what we do. If that were the case, it wouldn't matter what we did. But God changes too! God changes in response to what we do. In fact, God readily changes. God desperately wants to provide the very best for everyone in every city. Yet God depends upon people. If people get in the way of what God wants, God will find yet another way to try to bring about the good.

MEDITATION: Look around you, appreciating the sights and sounds where you are. Pay attention to the solitude . . . or to the people who are around you. Become observant of your environment.

Now close your eyes and let yourself, in your imagination, see and hear an environment that concerns you. Allow a city, a country, or a crisis in a region to come to your mind. Visualize the people who are in this environment. See how they are behaving. . . .

In your imagination, go to that place, walk through it, making a pronouncement: Tell them what is going to happen if they continue with their current ways. . . .

Now move to a spot where you can observe these people as they react to you. See how they respond. . . . Imagine them now showing signs of repentance—they are changing their ways. . . . Visualize how they can give up their wrongdoing toward one another and the earth. . . .

Imagine God's response to their changes. What does God do? As you observe, interact with God in any way you choose. Sit quietly, observing the scene before your eyes in your imagination. . . .

Now pay attention to the environment where you are physically. Hear again any sounds; open your eyes to see your environment. Notice your experience: what you appreciate, what you judge, how you repent, what you can change, and how you think God is responding. Sit quietly for a while.

COMMENTS ON DEBRIEFING AND USE: This meditation is a good example of the intersection of prayer and social action. It is difficult to sustain social action unless we have some hope that results can issue from our speaking or acting. Visualizing responsiveness, repentance and change in behavior toward positive ways, and God's bestowing bountiful grace can be most encouraging. A focus on positive images helps us sustain our action. Also, our prayer is more expansive when our prayer concerns are "big enough," not self-centered but self-transcending.

We may have to face situations in our world where humans do not react as well as the Ninevites did. We see no repentance in sight. Our debriefing, alone or with a group, may include some grief and sadness that the human population is slow in getting certain messages. Yet we can still hope! A God who can change God's mind and who has such clever teaching strategies will find some ways to catch our attention.

39

DECIDING WHAT MATTERS MOST

READING: "Again, the kingdom of heaven is like a merchant in search of fine pearls; on finding one pearl of great value, he went and sold all that he had and bought it" (Matthew 13:45-46).

BIBLICAL NOTE: See the BIBLICAL NOTE for Meditation 1 about "treasure stories." Finding the pearl first, then buying it, is like the one who finds the treasure in the field first, then buys the field.

Merchants who sought fine pearls often made long travels from Palestine to the Persian Gulf or even to India.

FOR YOUR MEDITATION: Like Meditation 1, this meditation provides simple, positive images, which makes it good to use with those who are new to guided imagery or with a large group. Any hands-on "pearls" you provide can facilitate the experience. It's amazing how much more people learn and remember an experience when they use their sense of touch and get a chance to manipulate objects.

MEDITATION: Close your eyes; sit straight and comfortably. Take three slow, deep breaths to relax. . . . Now imagine yourself in a meadow or grassy area. . . . Feel the warmth of the sun moving through your entire being. . . . Look around to see what is there with you. . . . Notice the colors of the grass and foliage, if you see any. . . . Walk around to get a sense of the larger area. . . . Now you notice a path . . . and another path . . . and still another path. All the paths are gentle uphill slopes. . . . You become aware that you are searching for something of great value. . . . Following your intuition and God's guidance, choose a path, doing whatever is necessary in order to find that for which you are searching. . . . Let yourself experience any struggles or barriers along the way. . . . Also, bring in any help or assistance that you want. . . . Finally you find this thing of great value for which you have been searching. . . . Observe closely what it is. . . . . You discover that you must sell or get rid of everything else in your life if you are to obtain this one thing. . . . Become aware of your inner experience as you make that discovery. . . . If you do decide to let go of everything else, follow through with that exchange and go back down the path to the meadow, aware of your feelings. . . . If you decide not to make the exchange, then go back down the path to the meadow, remaining aware of your feelings about the decision. . . . Let yourself stay in the meadow for a while. . . . When you feel ready, open your eyes.

COMMENTS ON DEBRIEFING AND USE: Some who practice this meditation are grateful for discovering what matters most to them. Yet some are understandably frustrated by their inability to decide what matters or how much it matters. Do not feel that you have to push yourself (or others) to *have* to decide.

Introduce relativity by making or drawing a "string of pearls" of different sizes. Then write the various valued things on the different pearls.

40

ACQUIRING PEACE WITHIN OURSELVES

READING: When the Blessed One had said this, he greeted them all. "Peace be with you!" he said. "Acquire my peace within yourselves!"

"Be on your guard so that no one deceives you by saying, 'Look over here!' or 'Look over there!' For the seed of true humanity exists within you. Follow it! Those who search for it will find it."

"Go then, preach the good news of the domain. Do not lay down any rule beyond what I ordained for you, nor promulgate law like the law-giver, or else it will dominate you."

After he said these things, he left them (The Gospel of Mary 4:1-11, *The Complete Gospels*).

BIBLICAL NOTE: The Gospel of Mary, like the Gospel of Thomas (Meditation 45), is one of numerous writings that originated around the time of the four Gospels with which we are so familiar. When the Bible as we know it was compiled, a council decided which writings would be included, much as anthologies are put together today. The writings that were not included largely went unexplored until they were rediscovered and translated into modern languages in this century.

Only three fragmentary manuscripts of The Gospel of Mary are known to have survived into modern times: Two were third-century Greek fragments, and the third was a fifth-century Coptic translation. This gospel shows us how fluid and passionate some of the debates among the early Christians about the meanings of Jesus' teachings were. Mary Magdalene recounts a vision of Jesus' teachings to the other disciples. Andrew and Peter are not sure whether to believe Mary, but Levi defends her teaching, saying, "If the Savior considered her to be worthy, who are you to disregard her?" (10:9)

FOR YOUR MEDITATION: This meditation might help a group that is debating certain laws or rules about being a Christian, being ordained, or being in good standing. You could practice the meditation before or after such a discussion. It can be helpful as personal reflection, during a time of inner turmoil, or as an aid in sorting out values.

MEDITATION: Take a few deep, slow breaths, in and out, as you center yourself and find a calm position, a calm frame of mind. Now imagine yourself in some familiar setting. . . . Sense what it is like to be there. Notice where you are, how you are acting, how others are interacting with you.

Now hear the words Jesus told Mary to share, "Peace be with you!". . . "Acquire my peace within yourselves!"

Imagine yourself in that same familiar setting, acquiring peace within yourself. Sense what it is like to be there with the others who have peace within themselves too. Interact for a while, peace being among you all.

Now notice if there is any law or rule that tries to dominate, to get in the way of the peace within. . . . Simply notice what that law or rule is. You may see it written in bold letters or just have a sense of the law or rule. You may privately notice this or talk to others about it. . . . Take whatever time you need. . . .

Remembering the law or rule that tries to dominate, again imagine all those present as having inner peace. Take time to sense this shared peace within. . . . You can return to this image again whenever you choose. Now enter your fully awake state, notice your surroundings, aware of the "peace within you."

COMMENTS ON DEBRIEFING AND USE: The laws or rules, noted in the imagery, could be spread across a mural, a chalkboard, or entered into personal journals. Write about, draw, or share with someone how you experienced that inner peace and how others seemed to you when they were at peace.

41

God's Glory Shining over All the Earth

Reading:
> My heart is steadfast, O God,
>> my heart is steadfast.
>
> I will sing and make melody.
>> Awake, my soul!
>
> Awake, O harp and lyre!
>> I will awake the dawn.
>
> I will give thanks to you, O Lord,
>>> among the peoples;
>>
>> I will sing praises to you
>>> among the nations.
>
> For your steadfast love is
>>> as high as the heavens;
>
> your faithfulness extends
>> to the clouds.
>
> Be exalted, O God, above the heavens.
>> Let your glory be over all the
>>> earth (Psalm 57:7-11).

Biblical Note: Psalm 57 is a prayer for deliverance from personal enemies. The poet cries for help, expresses trust, explains the situation, prays, expresses certainty of being heard, then, in the verses cited here, closes with a vow of thanksgiving, sung in anticipation of deliverance.

In much of Israel's poetry, ill fortune does not ruin one's faith, nor does good fortune reduce the meaning of the prior misfortune. Persons express both the depths of despair and of rejoicing to God.

FOR YOUR MEDITATION: This meditation uses the image of light as a way of conceiving of "God's glory" being over the earth. Glory is a type of light; it is easier to visualize light.

Imaging light is a helpful practice. When we do not know exactly what to pray for, we can always imagine a situation immersed in light. Light evokes a sense of guidance, warmth, radiance, and intuition. Halos are light surrounding persons. We can visualize halos hovering over whole cities as we see these places in our mind's eye.

Because this passage refers so much to music, music in the background could enhance the practice of this meditation.

MEDITATION: Sit quietly as you become calm. Take a few deep breaths. . . . Now in your imagination, visualize looking out over the horizon of the earth just before dawn while it is still dark. . . . Note your surroundings, nearby and afar, as you look out at the horizon. Now the dawn begins. . . . You might notice imaginary music, which sets the mood for the dawn. The sun moves slowly upward to start a new day on this part of the earth. . . . Notice the increasing warmth of the earth as the sun radiates upon it. . . . Become aware of the darkness fading as the light increases. . . . Let the music, in your imagination, be responsive to the greater light.

In your imagination, accept the magical ability to move around the whole earth, to watch the dawn as it keeps occurring. . . . The horizon keeps changing as the sun dawns in one city and the next . . . over countryside . . . in one nation . . . the next and the next. Stay in touch with the warmth, the light, which starts the new day. . . .

When you see a particularly dark part of the earth, a part that is suffering, linger there awhile. . . . See the light of the dawn moving into that place. Imagine God's glory being there, in every nook and cranny. . . . Linger in as many dark places as you choose, watching the dawn. . . . Notice the music in your imagination as it occurs in the various settings.

In your imagination, move "over all the earth," seeing God's glory. [At this time, alone or with a group, you may name different countries or situations aloud, giving time to imagine that place bathed in God's glorious light.]

Now come again to your original horizon, filled with light. Experience that radiance moving through you as you radiate this presence out to the world—the reciprocal receiving and giving of light. . . . Rest, as you began, in silence, in peace. Notice any imaginary music. When you are ready, open your eyes.

COMMENTS ON DEBRIEFING AND USE: I have used this meditation as much or more than any in this book. I feel the greatest need to practice this imagery when I find myself preoccupied with or frightened about national, international, or environmental crises. When I begin to panic or think quite pessimistically, I feel an obligation to balance that concern for the world with an inner conviction that God's glory is shining, that the dawn of a new day is trying to break through. My visualization helps me stay in touch both with my need to act for urgent care and with a hope for God's glory to shine over the earth.

The meditation is a helpful resource for community gatherings, even so-called secular events such as "Earth Day." Since it is rooted in the Hebrew Scriptures, it is conducive to Jewish-Christian settings.

Try hugging a "Planet Earth" pillow while meditating, or looking at a map. Afterward draw a huge mural of your images. Or, with a group, create one large earth picture with various images drawn over that earth.

42

JESUS: WHO IS FAMILY?

READING: As they were going along the road, someone said to [Jesus], "I will follow you wherever you go." And Jesus said to him, "Foxes have holes, and birds of the air have nests; but the Son of Man has nowhere to lay his head." To another he said, "Follow me." But he said, "Lord, first let me go and bury my father." But Jesus said to him, "Let the dead bury their own dead; but as for you, go and proclaim the kingdom of God." Another said, "I will follow you, Lord; but let me first say farewell to those at my home." Jesus said to him, "No one who puts a hand to the plow and looks back is fit for the kingdom of God" (Luke 9:57-62; see also Matthew 8:18-22).

BIBLICAL NOTE: In Asia Minor at the time of Jesus' ministry, there were two primary valued social institutions: the city government (the *polis*) and the household (*oikia*). As the Christian movement grew after Jesus' death, the Christians' challenge to both of these institutions was a significant reason for resentment against them. By the second and third centuries, during a time of rapid growth in Christianity, the church was virtually the only institution that provided strong social bonding (a kind of modern "social security"). Services that the city government and household had provided for widows, for example, were now available in church communities. Earlier care of widows had been the province of the extended family.

The dead had been buried in family tombs. (If you go to Rome and visit the catacombs, you can see how they buried their dead in family spaces.) The household extended its influence and power even beyond death. Christians, following Jesus, radically challenged the meaning of "family," for they included those who were not in their household. In fact, a high percentage of inscriptions on Christian "family" tombs grant permission for burial to nonfamily members, in contrast to the traditional warnings against burying others in family tombs.[22]

Jesus was so set upon the reign of God for all and soon, that he did disrupt households. He elevated children, the lowest in the household, claimed women to be (and often treated women as) equal to men, and referred to those not in the biological family as brothers and sisters. For several centuries, early Christians followed his example to the dismay of many traditionalists!

FOR YOUR MEDITATION: Basically Jesus is saying that his hearers should think differently about their families. He is not so much saying that they should forget their families as that they should radically alter who they perceive to be "family." Families should extend themselves to include those who do not have families. Families should not be so tight that they care only about one another or the family estate or family name.

Since we still wrestle with these issues today, I suggest a good deal of discussion (or reflection) before practicing this meditation in a group or privately.

Jesus speaks of attachments that keep us from following him in discipleship. We do not need to (and should not) leave our families literally, without discernment and discussion with them, even for what we perceive to be a call from God. However, sometimes attachments to parents, children, siblings, or spouses do stand in the way of spiritual growth and responses to God's guidance. We may be the ones who need to let go or to follow where guided.

We also can be less attached to other things that keep us from Christian discipleship. For example, some church members prefer clean carpets to sheltering persons without homes or to providing daycare for children. That attachment stands in the way of following Jesus.

I recommend studying Pamela Couture's book *Blessed Are the Poor?* in connection with this meditation. It discusses the relationship of church and society to the poor in different eras, showing that what we believe about individual and communal responsibility makes a difference.

MEDITATION: Stretch, laugh, smile, yawn, breath deeply, then find a comfortable sitting position, upright and centered. . . . Visualize yourself with your family in a setting you find yourself in often. . . . Observe that setting in detail. Now, to your surprise, the Christ walks through your environment. If it seems appropriate for you, tell the Christ in some way "I (or we) want to follow you.". . . (If it does not seem appropriate, do not say this.) The Christ stops, then tells you what it means to follow, what it requires. Listen to what is needed. . . . Feel free to make any comments to the Christ. . . . Allow a response from the Christ. Other family members may want to speak too. Listen to them. . . .

Notice any things that get in the way of your family's saying, "Yes, we'll follow you." Observe what these are. . . .

You realize that the Christ is on the way. . . . Bid farewell or go along, attentive to your thoughts and feelings.

Sit silently for a while, recalling the requirements for following, the things that get in the way of saying yes completely, and your current reflections. When you are ready, open your eyes.

COMMENTS ON DEBRIEFING AND USE: List the requirements the Christ, in your imagination, gave your family for being followers. List any things that keep you from following wholeheartedly. If you are with others, discuss these. Feel free to disagree with the requirements. (What gets in the way for some may in fact help others to follow. That is, some may say that a particular relationship keeps them from being more charitable; others may say that particular relationships encourage them to become involved.)

Draw a "Family Tree" not historically rooted in ancestors but descriptive of current relationships. Who is your "family" today? So-called "single" people may see themselves as highly connected to others. You might title this drawing "All My Relations," or "Mitakuye Oyasin," a Lakota phrase, which indicates that we are all related. (The Lakota *all* reaches beyond people to include the earth and other living things.)

43

REUNION

READING: Now Jacob looked up and saw Esau coming, and four hundred men with him. So he divided the children among Leah and Rachel and the two maids. . . . He himself went on ahead of them, bowing himself to the ground seven times, until he came near his brother.

But Esau ran to meet him, and embraced him, and fell on his neck and kissed him, and they wept. When Esau looked up and saw the women and children, he said, "Who are these with you?" Jacob said, "The children whom God has graciously given your servant." Then the maids drew near, they and their children, and bowed down. . . . Esau said, "What do you mean by all this company that I met?" Jacob answered, "To find favor with my lord." But Esau said, "I have enough, my brother; keep what you have for yourself." Jacob said, "No, please; if I find favor with you, then accept my present from my hand; for truly to see your face is like seeing the face of God—since you have received me with such favor. Please accept my gift that is brought to you, because God has dealt graciously with me, and because I have everything I want." So he urged him, and he took it (Genesis 33:1, 3-6, 8-11).

BIBLICAL NOTE: Twenty years prior to this meeting, Jacob had obtained Esau's birthright through deceit; received the blessing from Isaac, their father; then fled. At this point the two brothers are meeting again and embracing in reconciliation. Jacob had just wrestled with God through the night, being transformed from Jacob "the supplanter" to Israel "the one who strives with God." Here he remains somewhat skeptical of Esau's open exchange of brotherly love and lack of concern for the gifts that he has brought to appease him. Jacob expects Esau to hold a grudge, but Esau demonstrates sheer joy at seeing him again.

FOR YOUR MEDITATION: In this meditation, you may want to focus upon a sibling relationship. If not, consider any person from whom you feel some separation due to disagreement or simply distance or time. The two who have been separated can practice this imagery simultaneously. A third person (even a counselor) can lead both of you in the imagery, or you can read the meditation, then practice it silently.

See Meditation 8 for more on forgiveness and reconciliation.

MEDITATION: Become centered and quiet as you take a few deep breaths. Let go of any tensions, concerns, or thoughts. . . . Imagine yourself to be in a field. Let yourself be there for a while, noticing in detail what it is like. . . . Notice if anyone is with you or if you are alone. . . . Now visualize a person coming toward you. As this person comes closer to you, you see that it is an individual from whom you feel separated or estranged. . . . Notice that this person is running toward you, eager to be reconciled, eager to greet you anew. . . . Be aware of your emotions. . . . Begin to move toward this person and note how you are moving. . . . Greet this person, perhaps embrace. Allow whatever needs to take place to occur between the two of you. . . . Be silent together or talk. . . . When you are ready, hold out a gift that you have brought him or her. Present this gift and permit the person to respond to you. . . . Allow an exchange to take place between the two of you. . . . See whether you can move on together in a sense of reconciliation. . . . If not, become aware of what barriers prevent this. . . . Remain silent for a while, then open your eyes.

COMMENTS ON DEBRIEFING AND USE: After practicing this meditation, you may decide to make contact with the person through a letter, call, or visit. If the person has died or is no longer available for physical contact, this meditation may enable you to carry on the conversation even though the person is not present. You can practice this several times with the same person in mind or try various relationships. The gift can be a symbol of the current status of your relationship. Draw a picture or share your feelings verbally with that person.

If you are practicing with the person in your meditation, it is fruitful to act out your images with that person.

44

CHRIST HAS RISEN!—AN EMPTY TOMB

READING: But on the first day of the week, at early dawn, they came to the tomb, taking the spices that they had prepared. They found the stone rolled away from the tomb, but when they went in, they did not find the body. While they were perplexed about this, suddenly two men in dazzling clothes stood beside them. The women were terrified and bowed their faces to the ground, but the men said to them, "Why do you look for the living among the dead? He is not here, but has risen. Remember how he told you, while he was still in Galilee, that the Son of Man must be handed over to sinners, and be crucified, and on the third day rise again." Then they remembered his words, and returning from the tomb, they told all this to the eleven and to the rest. Now it was Mary Magdalene, Joanna, Mary the mother of James, and the other women with them who told this to the apostles. But these words seemed to them an idle tale, and they did not believe them. But Peter got up and ran to the tomb; stooping and looking in, he saw the linen cloths by themselves; then he went home, amazed at what had happened (Luke 24:1-12; see also Matthew 28:1-10; Mark 16:1-8; John 20:1-10).

BIBLICAL NOTE: In the passage as told in Luke, the three women (and perhaps others) go to the tomb with supplies for burial but witness instead evidence of the Resurrection. They go to their friends, the other disciples, and tell them what they have just seen. The Gospel of Mark records that the women tell no one because they are afraid. The women had reason to be afraid. Simply being a follower of Jesus could mean persecution or ostracism, but a woman's announcing God's action would have been unexpected and very controversial.[23] In Luke, the women do tell but are not believed. Peter goes to check out the evidence.

FOR YOUR MEDITATION: Clearly this meditation is appropriate for Easter Sunday and the weeks shortly after Easter when we celebrate

Christ's resurrection. However, this powerful imagery is evocative throughout the year. Situations that seem to have brought one to the point of burial can be transcended. There is potential new life. As a meditation for an individual, this passage would be relevant when healing is sought, hope is waning, faith is unsure. Just as groups (such as summer Bible studies) celebrate "Christmas in July," so too you could celebrate "Easter in October" at a crucial transition or event.

MEDITATION: If possible, take a walk, move or sway; enjoy your bodiliness and your environment. Stretch, take some slow deep breaths, and find a comfortable seated position.

Now imagine yourself with some good friends in a familiar place like a home. You realize that you and your friends are sad, mourning a past event. Get a sense of your situation—how you feel, what you think, what are your obligations. With your friends or alone, visit a place where you can identify with loss or a crisis that brings you to mourning. . . . If you go to a place you recognize in your imagination, pay attention to your expectations—what you think you will see. . . . You arrive, and the crisis is over! The mourning is no longer needed. Resurrection has occurred! . . . What is your reaction? If you are with friends, what do you all decide to do? . . . Do you tell others or remain private with the news? . . . In your imagination go from this place back to the home where you started your imagery journey. . . . Recollect your mourning, your expectations, your surprise, and your decision whether or not to convey the news of resurrection to others. When you are ready, affirm amen!

COMMENTS ON DEBRIEFING AND USE: Sometimes this meditation will bring only images of the Christ or the biblical women. However, it is not unusual for a personal or communal sense of resurrection to occur. Drawing the hopeful images or concretizing them in some other form is helpful because it sustains the trust in the process of new life. It reminds you regularly that resurrection can occur.

45

EMPTYING: AN ABSURD IDEA?

READING: Jesus said, "The [Father's] imperial rule is like a woman who was carrying a [jar] full of meal. While she was walking along [a] distant road, the handle of the jar broke and the meal spilled behind her [along] the road. She didn't know it; she hadn't noticed a problem. When she reached her house, she put the jar down and discovered that it was empty (The Gospel of Thomas 97:7-14, *The Complete Gospels*).

BIBLICAL NOTE: A copy of the Gospel of Thomas was found in 1945 in Upper Egypt, part of the archaeological discovery of the large Nag Hammadi library. The translation we have in its complete form was written in Coptic, which is a translation of what was probably the Gospel's original language—Greek. From references in other books, the existence of the Gospel of Thomas had been known a long time. Thomas differs from the four Gospels with which we are most familiar because it does not seek to present the life of Jesus. It is known as a "Sayings Gospel," consisting of one saying after another attributed to Jesus. It is, for us, rather like the book of Proverbs, which also presents words of wisdom. In fact, scholars place the Gospel of Thomas in the Wisdom tradition.

It is clear to scholars that Thomas obtained its material from the same oral traditions that our familiar four Gospels relied upon—that is, this gospel was being written or compiled during the same period, which was about 70–100 C.E.. We do not know who gathered these sayings, though it was common to ascribe a gospel to one of the apostles to foster a sense of its reliability.

FOR YOUR MEDITATION: The concept of emptiness is important, especially in our time and culture, which seeks to "fill" every moment and every closet. Emptiness can lead to reevaluation, a crucial requirement if we are going to be even slightly environmentally and socially responsible. Yet the idea of emptiness frightens a number of people. I have asked what scares people about emptiness and received answers such as: "I'm used to holding on, to having things, to getting things. I don't know what it would be like to go in reverse." "It's just frightening to not be filled." "It seems somehow like failure, loss." These comments lead me to wonder whether emptiness is precisely what we should meditate upon, for many of us "stuff" ourselves with food and drink or choke out our lives with "filler."

While the other four familiar Gospels do not name the concept of emptiness, Jesus did tell the rich to give away what they had. He encouraged people to foster less attachment to their nuclear families and to be more open to welcoming strangers. He asked people to release their emphasis upon fulfilling the law, replacing it with attention to motivation. All of these teachings involve aspects of emptying.

After practicing this meditation, a number of people reported finding some value in emptiness that they had not recognized; or they changed their prior ideas about what emptiness may "hold." I like to point out the value of what is not in a donut, a vase, a pretzel, or a day without plans!

Nevertheless, it is wise to pay attention to the possibility that persons may balk at the imaged emptiness. Discussing the passage and ideas associated with emptiness readies people to practice. Never force participation.

MEDITATION: Take a few slow, deep breaths to relax. . . . Let go of any tensions or concerns and just sit. . . . Now imagine yourself to be on a road, at a distance from your home. . . . You are heading toward home, so you reach down to pick up a heavy, full jar. . . . Now walk home, carrying the jar. . . . Observe what you pass along the way and what kind of road it is. . . . Take all the time you need. . . . Now you are home. . . . You enter through the doorway, then you notice that the jar you have carried all the way is empty. Be aware of your feelings as you see the empty jar. . . . Now hear the words: *The kingdom of God is like this.* . . . Let yourself experience whatever you feel or think. . . . If you want to, bring the Christ or any person you choose into your home to talk. . . . Take time. . . . Notice what the jar is like now. . . . Do you feel any differently now than when you first noticed it was empty? . . . Bid farewell to the person with whom you were talking, knowing you can communicate again. . . . Sit quietly, aware of your feelings. . . . When you are ready, open your eyes.

COMMENTS ON DEBRIEFING AND USE: Sometimes it becomes clear while practicing this meditation that there are things in life that either we do not want or to which we are too attached. If either occurs, be sure to

164

affirm that this is only one meditation with *one* image for the present time. It would be essential to reflect a great deal more before instantly letting go of something important. Sometimes nothing will occur that needs to be released. Some people find that their jars remain empty; others refill their jars during the meditation with exactly what had been there. Still others put different things back into the jar. How people feel about those occurrences vary.

You could draw the jar as it was full and empty. You might draw your home and the path to see how you depict those. If the attachments involve other people, it might be wise to share your feelings with them. Remember, you can enter your imagery meditation again to give it a different ending or to carry it further.

Some creative and adventurous meditators may want to sculpt their own jars.

46

Anointing, Proclaiming, and Remembering

READING: It was two days before the Passover and the festival of Unleavened Bread. The chief priests and the scribes were looking for a way to arrest Jesus by stealth and kill him; for they said, "Not during the festival, or there may be a riot among the people."

While he was at Bethany in the house of Simon the leper, as he sat at the table, a woman came with an alabaster jar of very costly ointment of nard, and she broke open the jar and poured the ointment on his head. But some were there who said to one another in anger, "Why was the ointment wasted in this way? For this ointment could have been sold for more than three hundred denarii, and the money given to the poor." And they scolded her. But Jesus said, "Let her alone; why do you trouble her? She has performed a good service for me. For you always have the poor with you, and you can show kindness to them whenever you wish; but you will not always have me. She has done what she could; she has anointed my body beforehand for its burial. Truly I tell you, wherever the good news is proclaimed in the whole world, what she has done will be told in remembrance of her" (Mark 14:1-9; see also Matthew 26:6-13; Luke 7:36-50; John 12:1-8).

BIBLICAL NOTE: All four Gospels tell the story of this woman's anointing of Jesus. The Gospel of John depicts her as Mary of Bethany (a faithful friend of Jesus). In John, the event occurs six days before the Passover at the home of Lazarus. The Gospel of Luke depicts the woman as a sinner rather than a disciple. She bathes Jesus' feet with her tears and dries his feet with her hair, rather than anointing Jesus' head.

Biblical scholar Elisabeth Schüssler Fiorenza, who titled one of her books *In Memory of Her* in honor of this anointing woman, reminds us that "wherever the gospel is proclaimed and the eucharist celebrated an-

166

other story is told: the story of the apostle who betrayed Jesus." That's true. At many celebrations of the Eucharist, we hear the words: "On the night in which he gave himself up for us. . . ." We do not say, "A few days after he was anointed. . . ." Not only is the unnamed woman who prophetically anointed Jesus' head seldom mentioned, but when she is, her image is often colored by Luke's version, in which she is made into a sinner.

In the ancient days of Judaism, when a prophet anointed another on the head, it meant that the prophet perceived that the other would be a leader. This unnamed woman was acting as a prophet, giving a sign, saying by her actions, "You are the anointed one." Jesus knew what she was doing, that is why he said she would be remembered wherever the gospel was preached.

FOR YOUR MEDITATION: This meditation is ideal for Holy Week during Maundy Thursday worship, which recalls the Jewish Passover meal. Or an individual who is meditating throughout Lent may choose this meditation weekly.

Any time of year, as you consider your spiritual gifts or desire to be heard and valued (or to hear and to value), this may bring forth some clarification or experiential insight.

MEDITATION: Find a comfortable position, look around to get centered, then close your eyes and take a few deep, slow breaths. . . . In your imagination, sense a place where there is a table and people gathered to celebrate the Passover. Notice that the Christ is there with friends. Get a sense of what the meal is like, the conversation. . . . A woman comes into the room with a jar of ointment and then pours the ointment on the Christ's head. . . . Notice what the friends who are gathered say and do. Let them interact in your imagination. Now the Christ says, "Let her alone; why do you trouble her? She has performed a good service for me." Sense how the people react. . . . What is the woman's experience? Become the woman or one of the friends in your imagination. . . . Let the friends, the woman, and the Christ interact. . . . What gift do you have? How do others react to your gift? . . . How does the Christ respond? . . . As the meal concludes, watch the people leave. Interact with the Christ as you feel guided. . . . Find a way to say good-bye, knowing you can reenter this scene in the future. Become aware of your physical environment, then open your eyes.

167

COMMENTS ON DEBRIEFING AND USE: An excellent way to ground this meditation would be to use real clay to make a jar, like the one in the image. It could serve as a reminder of the woman's recognized and valued gift of prophecy or of your recognized and valued spiritual gift today.

In a group, anoint one another with oil. Or alone, anoint yourself (knowing yourself to be anointed by God). Name the spiritual gifts that are being recognized.

47

FOLLOW THE STAR TO OBSERVE BIRTH

READING: Then Herod secretly called for the wise men and learned from them the exact time when the star had appeared. Then he sent them to Bethlehem, saying, "Go and search diligently for the child; and when you have found him, bring me word so that I may also go and pay him homage." When they had heard the king, they set out; and there, ahead of them, went the star that they had seen at its rising, until it stopped over the place where the child was. When they saw the star had stopped, they were overwhelmed with joy. On entering the house, they saw the child with Mary his mother; and they knelt down and paid him homage. Then, opening their treasure chests, they offered him gifts of gold, frankincense, and myrrh. And having been warned in a dream not to return to Herod, they left for their own country by another road (Matthew 2:7-12).

BIBLICAL NOTE: Western Christendom celebrates Epiphany, the day the wise ones find Jesus, on January 6. The "Twelve Days of Christmas" begin December 25 and end on "Twelfth Night," the evening before Epiphany.

Bethlehem is just a few miles south of Jerusalem. It is the home of Jesus' ancestor David, the burial place of Rachel, and a prominent place in the story of Ruth, who is referred to in Jesus' genealogy. Herod the Great ruled from 37–4 B.C.E. both in Judea and Galilee.

The Gospel of Matthew frequently mentions paying homage. These gifts were expensive, a likely reason for their choice.

FOR YOUR MEDITATION: The star, diamond, sun, or source of light is often a symbol for the higher self, guidance, or God. In this meditation, the "star" will be in line with this symbolism. The gift that the wise men brought will be symbolized for you through whatever gift you create to bring on your journey.

MEDITATION: Take a few slow, deep breaths and let yourself relax. . . . Now get a sense of yourself walking along a path in a grassy meadow, plains region, or some familiar place. . . . Feel the warmth of the sun on a clear day. . . . Observe whether people are walking with you or whether you are walking alone. . . . Watch the sun slowly set, the sky's slowly getting dark. . . . Now look at the dark night sky. A star shines brighter than the rest. . . . Go, follow that star, aware of your feelings and thoughts. . . . Become aware that a birth of great value will take place beneath that star. . . . You are holding some gifts you can offer. Look at these gifts that you are carrying with you. . . . Now you see ahead a setting that is indeed below this star. . . . Walk slowly up to this spot. . . . Become aware that the Christ is being born. Talk with anyone whom you choose in the scene. . . . Offer your gifts and pay attention to the response. . . . Stay in this setting, experiencing the power of this birth event and reflecting on the presence of the star. . . . Finish whatever you need to. . . . Now say good-bye and move on, still aware of the events that took place and your experience. . . . Become aware of yourself and your surroundings. . . . When you feel ready, open your eyes.

COMMENTS ON DEBRIEFING AND USE: Clearly the practice of this meditation is likely to be most poignant during the twelve days of Christmas. It could be an integral element of worship on Epiphany Sunday. However, there are numerous times when recalling the divine birth and the bringing of gifts in recognition of that divinity can be significant for an individual or a community. For instance, one could weave this theme into the celebration of the sacrament of baptism.

Create or draw the gifts that you brought in your imagination. Draw an "Epiphany card" with one of your images on it. Perhaps you are aware of something's being born through you. Give the card to another as an announcement of the birth.

48

Extending Our Families

READING: Meanwhile, standing near the cross of Jesus were his mother, and his mother's sister, Mary the wife of Clopas, and Mary Magdalene. When Jesus saw his mother and the disciple whom he loved standing beside her, he said to his mother, "Woman, here is your son." Then he said to the disciple, "Here is your mother." And from that hour the disciple took her into his own home (John 19:25-27).

BIBLICAL NOTE: Here we get a glimpse of Jesus' intimate love for his family and his friends. He cared deeply to make a "new family," the family of God, in which all people would be bound together in a kinship of radical discipleship. He is caring for his mother and his friend, yet many commentators have seen the symbolic creation of a new family in this gesture of particular love; a new family "born at the foot of the cross," in which the past and future families join. In other words, a family is made both from genetic relationships and friendships based on faith.

In Mark, Matthew, and Luke, the women watch Jesus from afar. Here they stand so close that they can talk to one another. He says, "Woman, here is your son," and "Here is your mother," equally naming the responsibility one has for the other.

FOR YOUR MEDITATION: Today we have many types of families. It is enlightening to ask persons who they consider to be their family. Not only do we have siblings and stepsiblings, adopted grandparents and stepgrandparents, but some neighbors or live-in members seem more like family than blood relatives with whom we have little relation. This ambiguity about who is family actually makes us ripe for grasping Jesus' message about extending families.

While this passage is a crucial element of the Good Friday remembrance, the extension of families is relevant many times during the year. This meditation could be a significant part of premarital counseling, when

171

families are combining. When aging parents are entering a new living relationship—moving to a nursing home or into the home of a family member—this meditation could clarify issues as well as symbolize a new covenant. Also if a church is considering a new form of community ministry, this meditation could help express that commitment.

This meditation and Meditation 50 are the only ones that suggest joining hands. Simply consider that option for your circumstances. You may practice this prayer from the perspective of the one who asks others to be family or from that of the persons asked to join in a new family.

MEDITATION: (*Join hands with those near you.*) Take slow, deep breaths. Feel yourself being supported by that which is holding you up—the floor, a chair. Let it hold you. Allow the earth to support you.

Visualize yourself in some setting that is nurturing and warm. It may be outdoors or inside. . . . Notice sounds, fragrances, sights, textures, even tastes. . . . Consider your various relationships and allow to come to mind particular relationships that need to be joined more fully, joined as family. . . . The Christ is there with you. Take awhile to get clear about who is joining with whom to create this new family. (You may be observing this, or you may be one of the members.) In your mind's eye, see each person clearly. Notice what you appreciate about each person. . . . Now you hear the Christ name one of the persons, asking that one to care for the other. Get a sense of how that person will take responsibility for the new relationship. . . . Now the Christ names the other person, asking that one to care for the first. Again get a sense of how that person will take responsibility for the new relationship. . . . Imagine the new family's caring for one another. Take whatever time you need. If any more advice needs to be given, allow that to occur.

Now sense the web of relationships with all beings around the earth. Sense God's care permeating the whole family of beings; affirm amen.

COMMENTS ON DEBRIEFING AND USE: Consider practicing this meditation when a person is leaving, even during the process of death, although it need not be limited to that context. Sometimes new families are created without anyone's leaving.

Draw an imaginary "Family Tree" with any images that arise from the past or the future. Discuss how the new relationship differs from what has been up to this point. Discuss how the new family has continuity with the former relationships.

49

PREPARING A PLACE FOR US: SAYING GOOD-BYE

READING: "Do not let your hearts be troubled. Believe in God, believe also in me. In my Father's house there are many dwelling places. If it were not so, would I have told you that I go to prepare a place for you? And if I go and prepare a place for you, I will come again and will take you to myself, so that where I am, there you may be also. And you know the way to the place where I am going" (John 14:1-4).

BIBLICAL NOTE: In the ancient theology of Israel, God would be present in any place where God's name was called. This passage continues in that tradition and serves as a response to the question that was in the disciples' minds: *How will you be with us after you have left us?*

Jesus' answer is not just otherworldly. They are already where they need to be, if they are aware of God's presence here and now.

Preaching professor Kendall McCabe in *The Path of the Phoenix* states that this "hardly seems a funeral text. It is a text brimming with life!" He suggests that it is a text we can begin to live with now, even though it stays with us into the hereafter.

FOR YOUR MEDITATION: In the Christian year, logically you would practice this meditation during Lent, just before Easter. However, whenever one is wondering about life and death or the continuity of life phases, this passage may provide significant help. We can pray, thinking of the Christ and his leaving. We can also reflect upon someone who is dying or who has died recently as we pray. The leaving need not be death. It may be a type of death: divorce, change in physical health, change in jobs or relationships. Children could practice a modified version of this prayer when they have to say good-bye to friends—or even a house or neighborhood—because of a move.

I recommend that you practice this meditation only after some experience with other meditations. If this meditation is practiced within a group context, give each person time to share.

MEDITATION: Become quiet and take three slow, deep breaths as you relax and seek to let go of any thoughts, tensions, or concerns. . . . Now become aware of yourself walking in a meadow or some other warm, nurturing environment. Observe the grass: its color and fragrance. . . . Notice flowers, trees, or foliage. . . . Notice that it is a warm, bright, sunny day. Feel that warmth moving through your own body. . . . Notice whether anyone is with you there or if you are alone. . . .

Now begin to walk along a gently sloping path, sloping upward. . . . Observe the path: how you are walking, and what is along the way. . . .

Now you come to a dwelling. As you walk up to that dwelling, you see written above the front doorway, "In God's House Are Many Dwelling Places." You stand there, observing the outside of this house. . . . When you feel ready, walk into the house. . . .

When you have browsed through the various rooms, walk into any room you choose. . . . Pay attention to your whole experience while you are in this room. . . . Notice how you feel, your attitude toward the room, the details of the room. . . . Now observe who dwells in this room, someone to whom you have said good-bye or are saying good-bye. . . . Allow that person to be there now in this room. Interact with this person in any way you wish for as long as you want. . . . Now ask this person for some token—maybe a few words or a gift—that he or she can give you to keep. . . . Watch how this person offers this gift and how you receive it. If you choose to give a gift to this person, go ahead and do that. . . . Now say good-bye in any way that feels right for you. . . .

Go back to the entrance of the dwelling and observe if there is any other room you wish to enter. If so, go through the same process of observing the room, interacting with the person who dwells there, asking for and sharing a gift, and leaving. . . . When you feel ready, go back to the front door and say good-bye to the whole house. . . . Think back upon the rooms that you have visited and on the people and gifts shared. . . . Now walk out of the house and back to the meadow or warm, nurturing place. . . . Notice the gift or gifts that you have. . . . Allow yourself to feel again the warmth of the sun on this day. . . . Become aware of your surroundings where you are sitting and your body. When you are ready, open your eyes, affirming amen.

174

COMMENTS ON DEBRIEFING AND USE: The pastor at a funeral I attended used a guided imagery prayer based on this passage. It was quite effective; it gave the family and friends a chance to say good-bye to the person who had died. (I would recommend that the minister discuss this prayer option with the family before using it to assure the family's comfort level with the idea.) Sometimes we want to carry on dialogues with a person who has died; occasionally a person is unsure it is appropriate to do so. A meditation like this gives permission for the dialogue process, and it provides a beginning and ending context for the dialogue, clearly delineating the imagery from the daily reality.

Drawings or small constructions of any kind would be helpful follow-ups for this practice.

50

Farewell and Blessings: Live in Peace

Reading: Finally, brothers and sisters, farewell. Put things in order, listen to my appeal, agree with one another, live in peace; and the God of love and peace will be with you. Greet one another with a holy kiss. All the saints greet you.

The grace of the Lord Jesus Christ, the love of God, and the communion of the Holy Spirit be with all of you (2 Corinthians 13:11-13).

Biblical Note: The final sentences of Paul's second letter to the church at Corinth closes with a benediction. Although this benediction names what we know as the Trinity, the idea of a Trinity had not yet developed when Paul wrote. He was simply affirming the grace of Christ, the love of God, and the presence of the Holy Spirit within that Corinthian community.

The early church practiced an exchange of a holy kiss, though we do not know exactly how it was practiced. It was holy because all people within the church were saints; the kiss between saints would be a holy kiss.

For Your Meditation: This meditation is written with the expectation that the setting is a group; it could be within worship, or it could be with a family, class, or small group. If you practice this with a large group, alter the words to indicate that each person would say good-bye to *some* of those present, not all. Practice saying the benediction together before the meditation, so that all are familiar with it and can repeat it in unison. Feel free to adapt the meditation.

This set of images is the most abstract in this book. It would be best to have experienced some of the other imagery meditations before this one.

Meditation: Stretch, laugh, cry, yawn, yell, moan, sigh; express whatever is current and present for you. Then settle down, sit in a comfortable attentive position, and take a few deep, slow breaths. . . . Become aware of this group, and in your mind's eye, visualize each person. . . . Now hear these words, "Finally, brothers and sisters, farewell." Observe your feelings as you hear this. . . . You hear, "Put things in order, listen to my appeal, agree with one another, live in peace." . . . In your mind's eye picture members of the group living in peace, putting things in order. . . . You may imagine this to be tomorrow or ten years from now. . . . Now you hear, "The God of love and peace will be with you." Get a sense of each person as he or she acknowledges the presence of the God of love and peace. . . . "Greet one another with a holy kiss. All the saints greet you." Imagine greeting each person, saying what needs to be said or being silent as you bid farewell. . . . In your imagination, allow others to respond to you, to say what they need to say to you as well. . . .

When the group is ready, join hands and repeat together the benediction, "The grace of the Lord Jesus Christ, the love of God, and the communion of the Holy Spirit be with all of you."

Sit in silence.

COMMENTS ON DEBRIEFING AND USE: It is natural to want to share with each person what you said or did in your imagery. This is a good idea, especially if time permits. People often share important feelings or insights when there is just a little time left. (This sharing could easily take the session's entire time.) However, it may be that some things are finally never fully said. That is also a part of farewells.

If group members were able to visualize concrete images, you could create a group mural or banner. They could draw images of past experiences with the group on the mural, along with images of the future. However, since the scripture passage is abstract in its imagery, a number of people may have words rather than images. The mural could be a mixed-media creation, words being as acceptable as pictures.

Group members could write letters or postcards to one another, based on the experience of this meditation. These could be collected and mailed at a given date in the future.

Sisters and brothers, farewell.
Peace be with you.

Notes

PREFACE

1. A racially mixed group of ten men participated. They met two and one-half hours once a week for seven weeks, using the meditations. Chaplain Paul presented a paper on this project to the Conference on Crime and Rehabilitation through Religion in Jerusalem, 1994, concluding that a loving and cohesive group had been formed, though much follow-up is required when we help people attend to their spiritual and psychological issues.

   Gail Paul, "The Use of Biblically Based Guided Meditations in a High Security Men's Prison: A Program of Spiritual Growth and Healing," 12.

CHAPTER ONE

1. An excellent discussion of wishes moving through will toward decision is found in the classic book by Rollo May, *Love and Will* (New York: W. W. Norton, 1969).

2. Ann Ulanov is a contemporary Jungian who writes about the importance of imagery as a component of the religious life. Chapters 1, 3, and 4 in *Primary Speech* are outstanding. Ann and Barry Ulanov, *Primary Speech: A Psychology of Prayer* (Atlanta, GA: John Knox Press, 1982).

3. Martha Crampton, *An Historical Survey of Mental Imagery Techniques in Psychotherapy and Description of the Dialogic Imaginal Integration Method* (Montreal, Quebec: The Quebec Center for Psychosynthesis, 1974), 2–3.

4. Dr. Carl Simonton became known in recent decades for his work with patients diagnosed with cancer. As a radiation therapist, he noticed that the role of the will and the use of imagination affected healing. Therefore, he developed an approach to cancer treatment that combined traditional treatment methods with biofeedback, meditation techniques, hypnotherapy, and psychiatry, which was implemented first at Travis Air Force Base when he was Chief of Radiation Therapy Service. See O. C. Simonton, S. Matthews-Simonton, and J. L. Creighton, *Getting Well Again* (New York: Bantam Books, 1980).

5. Ann and Barry Ulanov, *The Healing Imagination: The Meeting of Psyche and Soul* (Mahwah, NJ: Paulist Press, 1991), 6.

6. *World Book Encyclopedia* (Chicago, IL: World Book, 1992), Vol. 2, 564.

7. Robert E. Ornstein, *The Psychology of Consciousness* (New York: Penguin Books, 1975), 66–68, 155–57 and Claudio Naranjo and Robert

E. Ornstein, *On the Psychology of Meditation* (New York: Viking Press, 1972).

8. What I have described here is what Gadamer calls a "fusion of horizons" between the text and one's life. A discussion of Gadamer's and Paul Ricoeur's views of the imagination and the Bible can be found in the section, "The Function and Authority of the Bible," *Faith and the Play of Imagination: On the Role of Imagination in Religion*, David J. Bryant (Macon, GA: Mercer University Press, 1989), 148–62.

9. Anthony Mottola, trans., *The Spiritual Exercises of St. Ignatius* (Garden City, NY: Image Books, 1964), 70–71.

10. Patrick Fanning, *Visualization for Change* (Oakland, CA: New Harbinger Publications, 1988), 3–4.

11. Three works are useful for those wishing to explore the use of imagery within Christian education or spiritual direction: Robert A. Johnson, *Inner Work: Using Dreams and Active Imagination for Personal Growth* (San Francisco, CA: Harper & Row, 1986); Kathleen R. Fischer, *The Inner Rainbow: The Imagination in Christian Life* (Ramsey, NJ: Paulist Press, 1983; Elizabeth-Anne Vanek, *Image Guidance: A Tool for Spiritual Direction* (Mahwah, NJ: Paulist Press, 1992).

12. This use of imagination is named "Couples Choreography" by family systems therapist Peggy Papp in *The Process of Change* (New York: The Guilford Press, 1983), 142–64.

   Christie Neuger suggests that the use of imagination in counseling has both explorative and healing possibilities that other forms of counseling do not. The imagination bypasses the censorship and the linear logic used in the verbal therapeutic mode. Christie Cozad Neuger, "Imagination in Pastoral Care and Counseling," in *Handbook for Basic Types of Pastoral Care and Counseling*, eds., Howard W. Stone and William M. Clements (Nashville, TN: Abingdon Press, 1991), 157.

   An excellent resource for the use of imagination in pastoral counseling is Valerie M. DeMarinis, *Critical Caring: A Feminist Model for Pastoral Psychology* (Louisville, KY: Westminter/John Knox Press, 1993).

13. The therapeutic approach named psychosynthesis provides literature for those who work with individuals as well as groups in therapy. See Piero Ferrucci, *What We May Be: Techniques for Psychological and Spiritual Growth through Psychosynthesis* (Los Angeles, CA: J. P. Tarcher, 1982) and Molly Young Brown, *The Unfolding Self: Psychosynthesis and Counseling* (Los Angeles, CA: Psychosynthesis Press, 1983).

14. Charles W. Garrett, *Anniversaring: Taking Care through One's Memories* (New York: Vantage Press, 1988).

15. Morton T. Kelsey, *God, Dreams, and Revelation: A Christian Interpretation of Dreams* (Minneapolis: Augsburg, 1974), 72.

16.   See the provocative Christology of Rita Nakashima Brock in *Journeys by Heart: A Christology of Erotic Power* (New York: Crossroad, 1988).

CHAPTER TWO

1.   See an excellent discussion of "Revelation" in Maria Harris, *Teaching and Religious Imagination* (San Francisco: Harper & Row, 1987), 60–77.
2.   See Thomas E. Boomershine, *Story Journey: An Invitation to the Gospel as Storytelling* (Nashville, TN: Abingdon Press, 1988). The headquarters for the Network of Biblical Storytellers is located at United Theological Seminary, Dayton, Ohio.
3.   Walter Wink, *Transforming Bible Study*, 2nd ed. (Nashville, TN: Abingdon Press, 1989) and Conrad E. L'Heureux, *Life Journey and the Old Testament: An Experiential Approach to the Bible and Personal Transformation* (Mahwah, NJ: Paulist Press, 1986), 102.
4.   See a thorough discussion of these models in Sallie McFague, *The Body of God: An Ecological Theology* (Minneapolis, Fortress Press, 1993), especially 89, 91, 97.
5.   John E. Biersdorf, *Hunger for Experience: Vital Religious Communities in America* (New York: Seabury Press, 1975), 24–27.

CHAPTER THREE

1.   Herbert Benson, *The Relaxation Response* (New York: Avon, 1976).
2.   Ann Faraday, *The Dream Game* (New York: Harper & Row, 1974) 138–41.
3.   John Dominic Crossan, "Stages in Imagination," *The Archaeology of the Imagination*, American Academy of Religion Studies, Vol. XLVIII, Number 2, 1981, 55.
4.   Jeremy Taylor, *Dream Work: Techniques for Discovering the Creative Power in Dreams* (Ramsey, NJ: Paulist Press, 1983); Jeremy Taylor, *Where People Fly and Water Runs Uphill* (New York: Warner Books, 1992); John A. Sanford, *Dreams: God's Forgotten Language* (San Francisco: Haper & Row, 1989); Morton T. Kelsey, *God, Dreams, and Revelation: A Christian Intepretation of Dreams* (Minneapolis, MN: Augsburg, 1974); Patricia Garfield, *The Healing Power of Dreams* (New York: Simon & Schuster, 1992); Stephen LaBerge, *Exploring the World of Lucid Dreaming* (New York: Ballantine Books, 1991); and Eileen Stukane, *The Dream Worlds of Pregnancy* (New York: Quill, 1985).
5.   For several decades, Gestalt therapy has excelled at this identification with parts of an image scene or dream. See Frederick S. Peck, *Gestalt Therapy Verbatim* (Lafayette, CA: Real People Press, 1969).

THE MEDITATIONS

1. Mark Trotter, *What Are You Waiting for?: Sermons on the Parables of Jesus* (Nashville, TN: Abingdon, 1992), 38.

2. Carol A. Newsom and Sharon H. Ringe, eds., *The Women's Bible Commentary* (Louisville, KY: Westminster/John Knox Press, 1992), 258.

3. William A. Beardslee, et al., *Biblical Preaching on the Death of Jesus* (Nashville, TN: Abingdon Press, 1989), 115.

4. Edward Wimberly, *Prayer in Pastoral Counseling: Suffering, Healing, and Discernment* (Louisville, KY: Westminster/John Knox Press, 1990), 45–49. Wimberly shows how a woman in counseling stops identifying with the majority to side with the minority report, thus gaining a greater sense of strength to act and believe in her worth.

5. John Patton develops this theme in "Forgiveness, Lost Contracts, and Pastoral Theology," *The Treasure of Earthen Vessels: Explorations in Theological Anthropology*, eds., Brian H. Childs and David W. Waanders (Louisville, KY: Westminster/John Knox Press, 1994), 194–207.

6. Cindy Stackpole, Central New York Annual Conference of The United Methodist Church, reported to me orally, winter 1995, about a gathering of colleagues in Syracuse, New York.

7. Thomas Dozeman in Marion Soards, Thomas Dozeman, and Kendall McCabe, *Preaching the Revised Common Lectionary: Year B after Pentecost 2*, 20.

8. Sallie McFague, *The Body of God: An Ecological Theology* (Minneapolis, MN: Fortress Press, 1993), 142.

9. Thomas Dozeman in Marion Soards, Thomas Dozeman, and Kendall McCabe, *Preaching the Revised Common Lectionary: Year C after Pentecost 1*, 20–22.

10. Kathleen A. Farmer raises and discusses these questions in *Who Knows What Is Good?: A Commentary on the Books of Proverbs and Ecclesiastes* (Grand Rapids, MI: Wm. B. Eerdmans, 1991), 52–56.

11. Jane Schaberg, "Luke," in *The Women's Bible Commentary*, Carol A. Newsom and Sharon H. Ringe, eds. (Louisville, KY: Westminster/John Knox Press, 1992), 288.

12. Ibid. Schaberg cites Fiorenza on this point.

13. I expand on this theme, using Vashti and Queen Esther as biblical examples, in my book *When You Need to Take a Stand* (Louisville, KY: Westminster/John Knox Press, 1990).

14. In *Prayer On Wings: A Search for Authentic Prayer*, I describe five styles of prayer; imagery is one and repeated phrases another. Some people use the various "I am" statements of Jesus as repeated prayers. For example, they repeat "I am the vine" for five or ten minutes daily for a month or

so. Then they shift to a different statement, repeating that daily for a period of time. If a person repeats phrases in this manner, weekly imagery prayer could supplement the practice and enrich it. Likewise, repeating the phrases could supplement the imagery.

15. Elisabeth Schüssler Fiorenza, *In Memory of Her: A Feminist Theological Reconstruction of Christian Origins* (New York: Crossroad, 1983), 124 and Marion Soards, Thomas Dozeman, and Kendall McCabe, *Preaching the Revised Common Lectionary: Year B after Pentecost 1*, 83–85.

16. One suggestion for a book on massage is George Downing, *The Massage Book* (New York: Random House, 1972).

17. Kendall K. McCabe, *The Path of the Phoenix* (Lima, OH: C.S.S. Publishing Co., Inc., 1986), 19–20.

18. Antoinette Clark Wire, *The Corinthian Women Prophets: A Reconstruction through Paul's Rhetoric* (Minneapolis, MN: Fortress Press, 1990), 123.

19. Newsom, Ringe, *The Women's Bible Commentary*, 268–69.

20. Newsom, Ringe, *The Women's Bible Commentary*, 260.

21. Thomas Dozeman in Marion Soards, Thomas Dozeman, and Kendall McCabe, *Preaching the Revised Common Lectionary: Year B Advent/Christmas/Epiphany* (Nashville, TN: Abingdon Press, 1993), 120–22.

22. Dennis Ronald MacDonald, *The Legend and the Apostle: The Battle for Paul in Story and Canon* (Philadelphia: Westminster Press, 1983), 49.

23. Thomas E. Boomershine, *Story Journey: An Invitation to the Gospel as Storytelling* (Nashville, TN: Abingdon Press, 1989), 179–88. Boomershine points out that from Moses through the prophets, with the exception of Deborah, men were called to deliver God's messages to the people. I would add that it was men who were *heard* to deliver God's messages to the people. That is one reason the women were afraid (if they were). People might not *hear* that they were *called* to deliver God's message.

Index I: MEDITATION TITLES

The numbers refer to the meditation number.

Index II: BIBLICAL PASSAGES

The bold numbers refer to the meditation number.

Index III: SUGGESTIONS FOR USE IN DAILY LIFE

The numbers refer to the meditation number.

Occasions

Closing prayer at a meeting or in a group (best if you have time for debriefing): 2, 4, 5, 17, 18, 23, 29, 44, 46, 48, 49, 50

Crisis: 2, 6, 7, 8, 10, 11, 12, 15, 22, 24, 25, 26, 32, 34, 37, 40, 41, 43, 48, 49

Evening meditation: 3, 4, 14, 31, 39

Morning meditation: 2, 3, 7, 12, 27, 47

Opening prayer at a meeting or in a group: 1, 2, 8, 10, 12, 18, 25, 27, 30, 36, 41, 45, 46

Social Action and Transformation: 5, 6, 17, 19, 22, 25, 29, 33, 36, 38, 39, 40, 41, 42, 46, 48

Table grace: 9, 33

Vacation: 1, 10, 16, 17, 45

Groupings

(While most meditations are appropriate for all of these settings, those listed are especially well-suited to the various settings.)

Alone: 1, 4, 6, 7, 11, 16, 18, 21, 22, 24, 25, 27, 30, 33, 34, 35, 42

Family: 8, 14, 17, 19, 20, 21, 37, 42, 43, 47, 48, 49, 50

Large group: 3, 9, 12, 17, 23, 31, 32, 33, 41, 44

Small group: 2, 5, 10, 13, 15, 17, 18, 19, 22, 23, 27, 28, 29, 32, 34, 36, 38, 39, 40, 45, 46, 49, 50

With a friend: 8, 16, 20, 25, 26, 28, 43, 45, 48

Index IV: Suggestions for Use in Worship

The numbers refer to the meditation number.

Order of Worship

Call to Worship: 34
Invocation: 34
Prayer of Confession: 14, 28, 29, 31, 39
Words of Assurance: 21, 34, 45
Prayer of Confession *and* Words of
 Assurance, combined: 8, 13, 19, 20, 38,
 40, 43
Affirmation of Faith: 6, 18, 29, 42, 44
Prayer of Thanksgiving: 17, 30, 33, 35
Prayer of Petition or Intercession: 6, 7, 11,
 15, 24, 25, 26, 32, 33, 36, 37, 41, 48
Offertory: 8, 9, 12, 46, 47
Communion, Eucharist: 3, 10, 23, 33, 34
Benediction: 49, 50

Special Worship Settings

Baptism: 12, 17, 19, 29, 45
Christmas: 12, 27
Concern for the World: 5, 6, 17, 19, 22,
 25, 29, 33, 36, 37, 38, 39, 40, 41, 42,
 46, 48
Confirmation: 2, 12, 17, 19, 21, 29, 30, 34,
 39, 40
Dedication of a Building: 9, 12, 14, 18
Easter: 44
Epiphany: 47
Funeral, Memorial Service: 6, 10, 11, 18,
 25, 34, 42, 49, 50
Good Friday: 48
Graduation: 6, 12, 18, 21, 29, 30
Ordination: 2, 5, 6, 12, 17, 18, 21, 29, 40
Recognition of teachers, youth, students,
 etc.: 4, 9, 12, 15, 17, 20, 21, 23, 27,
 29, 42
Weddings: 2, 10, 15, 16

Index V: Symbols and Names

The numbers refer to the meditation number.